Open Midnight

Brooke Williams (signature)

Brooke Williams

Open Midnight

Where Ancestors
&
Wilderness Meet

Trinity University Press ◆ SAN ANTONIO

Published by Trinity University Press
San Antonio, Texas 78212
Copyright © 2017 by Brooke Williams

Cover design by Rebecca Lown
Book design by BookMatters
Cover art: *Head of Sinbad Galaxy*, by Bret Webster

Page 64: Ledger from the *Cynosure*, British Mission Emigration
          Register, pages 333 and 329.
Pages 130–31: Fernand Cormon, *Cain* [PD-US], via Wikimedia
          Commons.
Page 188: "I think" from Charles Darwin's Journals, Darwin's
          Notebook B, 1837. Reproduced by kind permission of the
          Syndics of Cambridge University Library.

ISBN 978-1-59534-803-6 paper
ISBN 978-1-59534-804-3 ebook

CIP data on file at the Library of Congress

21   20   19   18   17   ❖   5   4   3   2   1

For Terry

>The only stories I need,
>
>of grace and love and truth and wild beauty,
>
>you told me.

And Rio

(2001–2015)

>Joyful, joyful, joyful,
>
>as only dogs know how to be happy
>
>with only the autonomy
>
>of their shameless spirit.
>
>—from "A Dog Has Died," by Pablo Neruda

Contents

The doors to the world of the wild Self are few but precious. If you have a deep scar, that is a door, if you have an old, old story, that is a door. If you love the sky and the water so much you almost cannot bear it, that is a door. If you yearn for a deeper life, a full life, a sane life, that is a door.

—*Clarissa Pinkola Estés*

Author's Note

There is a ghost in this story. His name is William Williams, who is a real person. Very little is known about him. What is known about him comes through Mormon Church records: his family's transatlantic voyage aboard the *Cynosure*; as a member of the Rosel Hyde Company migrating across America; his unpaid loan from the Mormon Perpetual Emigration Fund; the personal history his youngest son wrote decades after his death. Based on this information, I am sure about these details of his life:

- The day he was born in Shrewsbury, England
- The birthdays of family members
- That, professionally, William was a joiner in the making of furniture
- The days different members of his family were baptized into the Mormon Church
- That he and his wife borrowed from the Mormon Perpetual Emigration Fund
- The day he left Liverpool, England, for America with his wife, Mary, and youngest son, John George

- ❖ The day he died at Three Crossings of the
  Sweetwater, Wyoming
- ❖ There were icebergs

Can a handful of dates tell the story of a life? In my mind these days are points along a line that, in this case, spans the fifty-five years lived by William Williams. The first things I see are the spaces between those points. If those points were stars in the sky, we would connect them to make constellations, which is what I've made with his life by creating the parts missing from his story. Whenever I've done this, I've been as true to the trajectory formed by the actual points, the real dates. While I'm not sure that what I've written into his life happened, I'm not sure that it didn't. It all could have happened. When I've woven his story together with that of Charles Darwin, I've been true to elements of Darwin's story, which is much better known.

Which brings me to this: I had help filling in the space between dots, completing the constellation. As I now believe to be true of all our dead, William Williams is out there in some other, perhaps quantum dimension, where he's found ways to influence me but only when I've been filled with enough wonder. He's been there when I made decisions that didn't make sense until much later. There have been times I've heard ideas, statements, possibilities come out of my mouth that I didn't understand, only to have them turn out to be true. Or when something unusual attracted my attention, which then took on archetypal meaning.

"You're making this up," you say. Perhaps. If so, I am making this up from elements lying dormant in my unconscious, which many believe may be much more vast, dense, and valuable than my conscious mind. And, perhaps, it is within the unconscious that all our dead continue to dwell.

Think about this: the dead far outnumber the living. Since they know the answer to the universal question of what happens when we die, imagine that they have answers to many other unanswerable questions. And, for me, it is easy to assume that they want to help us.

San Rafael River, Utah

Blinding afternoon sun fills the cab of our truck the moment we drop off the rim of the San Rafael Desert. Crawling down the gash in the cliff the map shows as an improved road, we manage to avoid the deepest ruts and largest rocks. This is December, the end of the year we've spent exploring the Great Wilderness. The Great Wilderness is the 10 million acres of iconic, mysterious, prehistoric, red rock desert in southern Utah. It is also the darker, vaster, more mysterious, more wild, even older inner world I once believed could only be accessed by dreams.

Though the map shows a crossing at the San Rafael River, we can't find it. We get out and check Ford for damage—dripping fluids, flat tires, new dents. Finding none, we start walking along the river, trusting that the map is correct—there must be a crossing nearby.

Finding none, we walk up a hill for a better view in the dying light, beyond the creaking sound of the truck's engine as it cools.

"We" refers to myself and Rio, my African Basenji dog-brother, and William Williams, an ancestor who died in 1863. Ten years ago he penetrated the thin veil between this life and that one and has since been my constant companion.

This is my last trip as field advocate for the Southern Utah Wilderness Alliance. What have I learned?

While driving or walking the loneliest, muddiest, ruddiest, godforsaken roads anywhere, I've learned that when the subject is Wilderness designation, the information on official maps doesn't always conform to what is found on the ground. I've learned that "ground-truth"— what I do all day—is a verb, but it is also a noun. It is the truth bubbling up through the ground like an invisible volcano or geyser from somewhere deep in the earth. I've learned that these ground-truths are better heard and felt in wilderness. During condensed time alone in these vast, quiet places, I've learned that magic happens. Magic happens in that for the first time since childhood, I experience events, sensations, and even visitations for which no intellectual explanation exists.

I have what I've come for: firsthand knowledge that this route ends here and does not, as the map suggests, cross the river. But I've learned that what I've come for is a small part of all there is.

For most of my life, I'd quit, turn around, go home, once I had what I'd come for—found the bird or the river or seen the view from the summit, or gathered the route information I needed. Now, I wait for the rest of it. I wait for the inner world to reveal itself.

Some think that everything evil and dark lurks in this inner world and sealing it off is necessary for maintaining civility. Others believe that this inner world holds the clues to the survival of our species. Magic happens in the wilderness because in this wild, remnant system vibrating in place since those first exploding stars, the membrane separating the outer and inner worlds thins and, at times, dissolves completely. For me the inner world opens in the wilderness.

Based on what I've learned, we're crazy not to look inside for answers, especially during these times when economic, cultural, and climatic shifts threaten life as we know it. When everything we depend on is at stake.

I wait. Winter silence floods the space freed when the rugged road and my old truck no longer need my attention. Facing the long and vacant view, I feel the story begin to move.

This is my story, but it is also the oldest, shared story about passing life onto the future. It may be that we need this story now more than ever. It is time for this story.

I need wild silence to hear the story. The wilderness is where I sense pieces of the story. The story is a puzzle. I think the story is always here, playing as if far away someone is singing.

On the canyon wall to my right, the sharp line separating sun and shadow has climbed two feet in the few minutes I've been standing here wondering what to do next. I have food and sleeping bag and a lighter and water. That things didn't go as planned today and the high possibility that the temperature will sink below zero tonight aren't likely to have serious implications. But only if I don't go ahead and do something stupid. Like try to drive my truck across the San Rafael River.

Other options are to attempt to turn my truck around in this tight space and loose sand and drive it back up the way I'd come, or to camp here and hope something changes by morning, which never really works. A slight breeze rises, and the musky sweet smell of moving water overcomes the frozen stillness.

"So, Rio, looks like the end of the road," I say out loud, my words like bells ringing in the silence. "Either we camp or we drive hours in the pitch dark, back the way we came." I can tell by the look on his face as he sits there in the cold sand that he wants to drive on.

For forty years I've lived under a spell I can neither explain nor ignore. I've both needed and loved being outside in the wilds. As if I'm protected by an invisible force, I've always been repelled by any situation that threatens to keep me out of the wilderness. Fortunately, I've always had good work and have never been hungry or cold except by choice or personal oversight.

In all those years, wilderness has been under constant threat. In one way or another, I've been involved in efforts to protect and defend wilderness, and on the constant lookout for new strategies or methods or some fresh source of reasoning.

Lately this has all changed. My point of view has shifted. Where I once spent my creative energy on new strategies to use in saving wilderness, I know now that the wilderness saves us. While I don't know for certain that William Williams had anything to do with this shift, I don't know that he didn't. I do know that the timing of this coincides with his showing up in my life.

This place—the San Rafael Desert—is not popular in the way that the San Rafael Swell and many places within a hundred-mile radius are. It has none of the scenic or iconic sandstone spires or arches; none of the mythic deep, sensuously curving canyons. But wildness isn't necessarily scenic or iconic. I'm betting that in the future, we'll still value what's scenic and iconic, historic, and ecologically important, but it will be the solitude we'll value most. We will seek out wilderness for its silence, its absence, deep and dense enough to become presence, that it will be impossible to find anywhere else, that we'll travel days looking for and hoard once we find. In a future insisting that we constantly communicate, technology will absorb our lives. This desert—this wilderness—with its intimate and infinite views and exposed bones and blankets of sage and ancient grasses, will be the only place left to hear our true selves think.

I pull the lever putting my truck into four-wheel

drive and, shifting from reverse to first to reverse eight times in the narrow space, face back the way we've come. I'm surprised how easily my truck climbs the steep pitch, and we're back on the rim in minutes, in time to watch the yellow sun ball melt across the horizon before evaporating out into the cold night.

We drive a mile, then two, the gray light darkening toward black. On top of a small rise, Rio gets restless. I stop in the middle of the frozen road and let him out. Sitting in Ford's cab, the heater cranked to high, I hear Williams's familiar voice: "Get out. Turn off the lights. Look around."

I do. Pummeled by the cold, I zip my parka and pull my hat over my ears. Looking out, first two stars appear, then six. Minutes pass and then there are dozens. I stand there marveling about the 200,000 years that our ancestors stared out at the stars, wondering about the knowledge they absorbed from the night sky. What are we missing now when, because of increasing light pollution, only 10 percent of people on the planet can see the Milky Way?

For me, this story began with one question: How can we protect more wilderness? While looking for answers, I discovered hidden within that question two more questions: Why do I care about wilderness, and during these trying times, how is wilderness important?

The answers, I've discovered, are found in one phrase: "Open midnight."

Early one morning last spring I was half-asleep, the

desert coming alive outside sending the smell of rain and green through the open door. Stacked on the lamp table next to my bed were all the books I'd been reading, hoping for answers to all my questions. "When the books are gone, open midnight" echoed out from a corner of my room.

The word *midnight* has many meanings. We're taught to believe it is the dark world we enter in sleep when all the demons come alive. It is halfway between dusk and dawn, but also between where we've been and where we're going. For me, midnight represents the unconscious, that huge place where all possibilities are hidden. Open it, and like a once-locked room in the back of your house, find everything you need. Walk in and become fully awake.

This both excites and terrifies me because knowing how to become fully awake demands that I attempt it— not doing so would be cowardly and unfair.

Parts of the sky have more stars than spaces between them, I see, as I pee out into the night. It's damn cold and so still and I feel the entire universe screeching to a halt. If I get dizzy and tilt to one side, I will not fall in this air that silence has made as dense as water.

I'm comfortable not knowing what exactly it is that I'm feeling out here in the middle of nowhere, nothing but a frozen road to suggest that I'm not the first person ever to stand in this huge presence. I realize that I'm comfortable because whatever is happening to me in these situations is not coming in along that path from my eyes or ears or nose to my brain where it gets processed and explained. It is being forced through every pore in my skin, entering directly into my bloodstream.

This may be how the story feels. But this is not the story. The people I trust most, those I work with, and my best friends all know how the real story feels. We've been able to protect wilderness by learning the political, legal, and economic systems.

"But why does the wilderness save us?" This is the story we need.

"Learn to tell the story." This is what I hear the ground saying to me. "Learn to write it. And then learn to say it out loud."

On Highway 24, the green numbers of the clock on my dashboard tell me it's eight o'clock, meaning we've been backtracking nearly two hours, that we're still two hours from home. The small headlight-lit world I can see is safe and straight, but beyond it lays the dark, rich world where all possibilities sleep.

My story begins one night on a river trip down the Colorado. We were camped at the mouth of a small side canyon near the confluence with the Green River in the middle of Canyonlands National Park. I've spent five hundred days hiking and camping in wild canyons, named and unnamed—all part of the Colorado Plateau's circulatory system. I'd rafted down all the major rivers.

That particular trip down Cataract Canyon stands out for three reasons: because it was the longest I've ever been out—over a month; because at times we felt like John Wesley Powell himself, wandering in places without any sign that we weren't the first white people ever to set foot there; and because that evening in that side canyon I discovered something significant I would later identify as my own inner world.

I had graduated from college the prior spring. Although I felt prepared, I wasn't ready to step into the real world. If the "real world" was a pool, I'd already put a toe in and didn't like the feel. It was October and we'd planned for the long nights by bringing extra batteries for our headlamps and a large ammo can full of books. I'd barely started *The Lion, the Witch, and the Wardrobe* when I began obsessing about it. My banter became relentless and my fellow travelers demanded to read the book to get to the source of my passion. We had only one copy so I tore the book into four equal sections.

The first tear was difficult—opening the paperback approximately a quarter in, holding the top of those pages in one hand, the rest in the other, and pulling down gently enough so as not to destroy it, yet hard enough to overcome the strength of the spine.

John and Tommy, two friends from college turned professional river guides, had invited me along on an off-season private trip. Ote (short for Coyote), Bego (short for I don't know what), and Melissa—also river guides—

were friends of theirs. We didn't talk about it, but we all needed to escape. We weren't desperate.

Our plan was to run Cataract Canyon. Typically a five-day trip, our escape would last a month, although we didn't know it at the time. As is true on all river trips, by day three it was obvious that all we needed in life was that raft, a handful of good people, enough fuel to keep us going, and books. Besides *The Lion, the Witch, and the Wardrobe* our library contained some history of the area, field guides to the birds, bushes, and trees, some Ed Abbey—*Desert Solitaire* and one of his novels, *The Brave Cowboy.* Also in that can was a giant folded topographic map of Canyonlands National Park for the exploration we would do along the way.

By day three I'd nearly finished the book. I dream better at night in the wilds, but the book was like a dream too, and night meshed with day. I suggested we name the trip "Narnia." I'd never named a trip before.

I wrote "NARNIA" in bold blue letters across the top of the map.

By day ten we had become the river. We moved like the river. We and the river were the same red-brown color. If we'd had a schedule, we were on it. We were tan and strong and happy. We'd all finished *The Lion, the Witch, and the Wardrobe* and modified our map accordingly, re-naming features, noting what we'd seen and found—all we'd thought and felt.

Like many explorers before us, we'd hiked nearly

every side canyon on both sides of the river looking for a route west. We needed a way through the many vertical sandstone and limestone formations between the river and the rim. I don't remember why. That afternoon we camped at the mouth of a canyon, which, on the map, showed promise. We started hiking late and it was nearly dark by the time we'd reached the base of the last cliff. Though dusk turned the air purple, we could make out where the vertical wall was broken into a jagged line of boulders, which could be our route to the rim.

Walking back, feeling our way through the pure, thick, and starless dark, the canyon came alive. We were no longer on the earth. We were in it. The canyon croaked and buzzed. The wildness pulsed, deeply, inaudibly. I'd wondered what powered my beating heart and suddenly I knew.

Something is going on, I thought. I kept this to myself, not wanting to appear foolish.

That night, back in camp, we marked up the map by firelight—with arrows, circles, and notes.

The next morning we noticed people camped across the river. Their presence reminded us of our dwindling food supplies and that our trip was taking longer than we'd planned. Bego and I got in one of our rafts and rowed over to meet them. They'd driven their rental car from Moab and hiked down to spend one night as part of their trip through the Southwest. They liked the idea of letting us hike out with them, taking us back to Moab for food, then dropping us off the next day at a point upriver. From there Bego and I would hike down a canyon we'd found earlier to the north, requiring one short rappel. We would swim the river, pushing ahead of us our Hefty bag–lined packs filled with fresh food and just enough air sealed in to keep them afloat. Once on the other side, we would climb a long ridge and then follow the rim to the top of the canyon we'd explored the day before. The crux would be finding the boulder-route back down the canyon to our camp.

Everything worked according to plan. We were partway up the long ridge—we'd done the rappel, the swim, and our food was dry—when suddenly I wondered about plan B, in case we couldn't get down from the rim. We had no plan B. Bego wasn't worried. We'd just go back down to the river and catch a ride to camp on the next boat. I didn't think about the possibility that next boat might not come by until April.

Getting to the gap we'd seen earlier required four dry hours in autumn heat, map reading, and complicated route finding. After two dead ends I knew we'd found the way when I felt the rising breeze carrying the same sweet air we'd breathed down below the day before.

I don't recall the details of getting down through that gap. What I do remember is being transported from a high, hot orange world with infinite views to a dark, cool green one. I remember feeling swallowed and the hair on my neck standing up.

That night, after pasta and fresh vegetables, we had a lot of work to do on the maps. This previously unnamed canyon would forever be called War Drobe Canyon, words we added to our map in dark blue pencil.

With both the book and the canyon, passing through the wardrobe was passing from the outer to the inner world, a world as least as rich and wild and more full of mystery than any part of my outer world.

Although I sensed something changing, years passed before I would realize that much of what I loved about being in the wilderness was because out there, my own inner wilderness becomes more accessible.

I struggled with this. I wasn't good at accepting anything that couldn't be proved, that required faith or belief. My background in field biology gave me the confidence to know that regardless of how magical or spectacular or impossible any element of the natural system seemed, there was a very logical explanation based in natural selection and the result of biological evolution.

Our species has a long history going back to that first slime coming alive in those steamy pools, and but for a few close calls we've done well ever since. That success has been based on a thousand different tools stored deep in our cells, many of which our terminal brains—the maximally highest-quality life-form nature will ever come up with—can't understand, let alone explain, and therefore has learned to ignore. At our peril.

If we do manage to save ourselves, to dodge the climate bullet now aimed directly at our collective forehead, we will credit an idea that today has either not yet been dreamed or seems too "woo-woo" and, therefore, foolish.

The "woo-wooians" just may be our best hope. Woo-wooians in the wilderness, even better.

I may never fully appreciate the importance of modifying that Canyonlands map. I hadn't thought about that 1974 river trip for years. But I trust stories to come back to us when we need them. The map of Canyonlands we took with us on that long-ago river trip was a map of the outer world: the blue lines indicating water, the green vegetation, the brown topography . . . and places named long ago, many for obvious reasons. Like all maps, one of its purposes is to provide points amid the nothingness where, because of the detail and our knowledge of how to read it, we were able to say with nearly complete confidence, "I know where I am."

We marked it up. We changed it according to our own experience. We added a different dimension, one based on our discoveries—what we found on the landscape, but also inside of ourselves. If read correctly, the revisions we made to the map could also read, "This is where I am."

That night, in that canyon, I first experienced the inner wilderness. The most important places in my life are those where holes opened up in the wall separating the worlds, big enough for me to move through. Many I would have missed had William Williams not been nearby to focus and direct me. Places—I'm convinced—each with a different piece of that one great story of life. This book is a series of points along my path toward knowing that this is true.

ONE

Castle Valley, Utah

Terry and I first came to Castle Valley in 1998 when one hot Saturday late in August we made one of those innocent decisions that ends up becoming life-changing. We were in Moab, Utah, for the weekend and one morning decided to drive to Castle Valley, twenty-five miles up the Colorado River. I'd been to Castle Valley once, years before. Before the weekend was over, we had contacted a realtor who showed us what seemed to be the perfect house. For five hours we drove back to Salt Lake, counting all the reasons we couldn't uproot and move after a lifetime living in one place. We could think of only two: a job and five generations of family history. By Labor Day we had sold our Salt Lake home and bought the one in Castle Valley. After some remodeling, we officially moved in on New Year's Day, 1999. It has been as if we opened a hidden door in our lives and discovered a room we didn't know was there.

Besides going away to school or on a mission for the Mormon Church, no one in my immediate family had ever made a conscious choice to live outside a fifty-mile radius of Salt Lake City. But then I'd always been the different one. "My most sensitive child" is how my father often referred to me, differentiating me from my four siblings. That's at the conscious level. Possibly at a different and unconscious level, beneath the surface of things, beyond the obvious, I often wonder if I'm the one in our family picked to be concerned about the future. Calling me sensitive may make the most sense to a fairly mainstream American family like mine. I guess I have always been *sensitive*—emotional even from a very young age—the kid with the temper. Growing up, I was always concerned for the other—animals or people of a different race or socio-economic status. Since high school I'd been focused on conservation of the natural world at one level or another. While there may be a dozen ways to explain how I was different growing up, that I was the one chosen to worry about the distant future may be as good as any.

It was the same with Terry. With three brothers in the family construction business, she became the self-proclaimed conscience. The first of nine grandchildren, Terry was mentored by her grandmother, Mimi, who set an example for her of an open, constantly learning, adventurous woman. From the first days of our marriage, Terry and I attracted mentors who showed us that loving the wild world meant both understanding it at its deepest levels and working to protect it.

For two decades before actually moving to the Colorado Plateau, I'd spent much of my free time exploring the most intimate and lost nooks and crannies, the wildest and least-known corners of this vast region—the last piece of America discovered by early Anglo explorers. I found that not everyone felt the way I did about all this beauty and wildness. Many of those living in the small communities scattered across the part of the Colorado Plateau that spilled into Utah had a different point of view. They saw the same wilderness, which I craved and needed nearly like a drug, as a source of timber and coal and oil to feed the insatiable American machine while providing their living. When we moved to Castle Valley, local and national efforts to protect these wild places were focused on legislation that would designate millions of acres of the public lands I loved as official Wilderness as defined by the Wilderness Act of 1964.

I couldn't imagine actually living in a place surrounded by the same wildness we'd visit during a dozen weekends each year for hiking, mountain biking, and skiing. For both Terry and me, being out in the wilds has always been much more than recreation. Moving through a wild landscape always stirs something deep inside us, something magic and old, like the heat from a small fire glowing in our chests. The opportunity to have that every day was the best of all miracles.

What we expected was just enough to get us through the mental and physical effort required to extract ourselves from fifteen years in one house and five generations in one place, akin perhaps to overcoming gravity on the way to outer space. This was small in comparison to what we got when we moved.

By moving to Castle Valley, we got a completely new life governed by rhythms and light, not clocks. We got fresh vegetables from the overgrown gardens of generous neighbors; snakes and spiders in our house (some of the spiders are poisonous, not the snakes); power outages; gale-force wind through badly latched doors bringing inside the fine red dust it has carved off the rocks; insect infestations (grasshoppers one year, cutworm caterpillars another). We rediscovered the word *red*, and we now know that like DNA, the letters RED are code for the universe of possibility we watch move in the cliffs, a wild and infinite spectrum with a pale beginning one step from white and ending late on a summer night, the second before black.

Castle Valley has no store, no gas station, one B&B, a fire station, a community center with a small library and a large room for the many community meetings. Like Sacrament Meeting, Relief Society, and Sunday School, these meetings were once held in the local Mormon Church between basketball practice, valley weddings and funerals, and monthly community potlucks. Unless you pay for satellite, television does not exist in Castle Valley. Without it, I've found a new capacity for paying attention—to the globe mallow blooming orange right before the prickly pear cactus blooms yellow; the dates when that first deer wanders across our land in the fall and the last leave in late spring; the different points on the cliffs where the sun rises as the year moves through time. Because we can't watch TV, we sit on the porch before dinner as the setting

CASTLE VALLEY, UTAH ♦ 21

sun darkens the cliffs. Now we read more. We go to bed earlier.

Community, we've learned, is not a group of hand-picked people living spread out across a big city who talk the same, read the same books, go to the same movies. Community is geographic. Community is people who decided to live in the same space, usually for very different reasons. Community is more like electricity than neighborhood, a force that when channeled can move governments. It is also the spotlight that shines on each member's flaws and strengths so everyone knows what they're working with.

According to geologists, Castle Valley is one of eleven collapsed salt dome valleys in the area. It formed when water flowing far beneath the earth's surface dissolved a deeply subterranean layer of salt and the sandstone and limestone on top of it crumbled and collapsed. I don't know whether this happened in one terrible, wonderful cataclysm or gradually over the course of hundreds of thousands or millions of years. Regardless, Castle Valley is now 10,000 relatively flat acres situated 300 feet below and between Wingate sandstone walls to the east and west. These walls are the raw edges of the crater formed when the valley collapsed, the low-lying Moenkopi siltstone to the north, and the La Sal Mountains to the south.

A neighbor who is a professional archaeologist thinks that the valley has always been used for hunting. There is evidence that the huge boulders in the hills at the base of the cliffs served as shelters for hunters. Every morning and late evening deer move across the valley like peaceful brown tides. We watch them pretending we are prehistoric hunters, waiting for them.

Archaeologists classify those who came to Castle Valley for deer and bighorn sheep as desert archaic—nomadic hunter-gatherers who lived before the Anasazi. We all have hunter-gatherer ancestors who appeared eons ago and continued that way of life until 10,000 years ago when agriculture was discovered. Physically, our human bodies have not changed since we lived as hunter-gatherers. Sometimes, I'll be running along with Rio and suddenly sense that ancient part of myself—I'll realize that I'm getting better at smelling deer and the air before rain, or feel the shifting breeze, or a foreign presence. It is just enough for me to feel frustrated and even a little cheated—as if all this knowledge is still inside me, inside all of us, like a perfect old violin no one remembers how to play. Still, I like to think that my getting to know my home range by regularly running through it with Rio is not so different than what the Native hunters were doing in Castle Valley five hundred years before Columbus.

Is it possible to become native to a new place? I wondered one morning, running along a deer trail east of our house. Rio was out ahead. This was one of a long train of thoughts that began earlier, the moment I picked up my shoes, signaling Rio. I'd been around him enough to believe that he doesn't necessarily "remember" what those shoes mean, as much as what those shoes signal to him via the hundreds or even thousands of his sensors reacting in concert to every situation. Once we were out on the trail, I decided to keep track of the "signals" the familiar landscape gave off to Rio. I made a mental map.

- ◆ There's the first barbed-wire fence. Rio always sniffs the bottom wire for information on who has crossed ahead of us. He goes underneath and disappears to the north while I hold the top wire down and climb over.

- ◆ I know he'll catch up just as I cross the first wash, which he darts through and up the other side. There was once a decomposed deer carcass ten feet off our path to the left of where it rises out of the wash. It's been gone for a year, but Rio still checks to be sure it has not come back.

- ◆ He finds a bone with a tendon still attached. With or without a bone, I know the exact point along our route where he will reappear. He is carrying the bone he discovered when he passed me.

- ◆ I knew I would find him chewing on that bone in the first major shade, the base of one of the few juniper trees along the route.

- ◆ I don't make it to the second wash before he catches me. I never do. We run up the far side together. We always do.

- ◆ On the other side, our route flattens and straightens.

I've come to expect Rio to disappear to the right while I find my stride. I don't know where he goes or why. I suspect there is another carcass or perhaps an old coyote den. Someday I'll follow him to find out. I'll run half a mile before I see him again when I make the turn toward the second fence, which we follow back toward the house.

◆ If I'd been keeping track, I'll bet Rio disappears at the exact fence post every time we run along this route. He heads north toward the road. I know he'll be checking the fenced dogs owned by two of our neighbors.

◆ Depending on how fast I'm moving or what else he finds during his detour, we may or may not arrive back home at the same time. Regardless, he'll run immediately to his water bowl for a drink, then perch on the rug beneath the dining room table, exactly like the pharaoh's dog statue we bought to remind us of him.

Rio is incorrigible when it comes to many things, but deer are his major weakness, or strength, depending on your perspective. All his signals are weak when compared to those that deer send him. Since he is too small to see over the sage, it is usually the smell of deer that triggers his huge hunting instinct. On occasion we will be trotting along on parallel paths, the barely perceptible breeze nudging us from behind, when suddenly the wind shifts to the side and fills with the scent of deer. Instantaneously Rio lunges to his left as if he has come abruptly to the end of a cable hooked to his collar. If he hasn't already bolted toward the scent, I shoot him with the harshest words I can produce: "Rio, stay." On the very rare occasion that he hears me, he might turn toward me with a look that says he has no control over what he is about to do. As if the brain he uses to process my words is no match for his blood. He takes off, boiling with instinct. He has yet to obey.

What is trying to signal me? Light, smells on the breeze, unique movements of specific birds or animals. I'm rarely conscious of them—too busy thinking about something far from where I actually am. I'm particularly aware of the signals birds send out. Often, I'll see a bird flash in the corner of my eye and before I've had time to think, I'll react to it. I'll mysteriously know it. The moth-like rhythm of its wings combined with its size, its relationship to the ground, the flash of its white rump—all registering in my body as "marsh hawk," a harrier, before my brain has time to respond. If there's a question, we stop to discuss it and even pull out the bird book. Nine times out of ten, I'll find that my first reaction was right. These signals must be bypassing my brain. I have realized how clear my signals are in Castle Valley, or in any wild place, and how muddled or absent they are in cities. Memory and thought are produced in my brain, while signals seem to be wild elements from the landscape directly entering my nervous system in the form of instinct.

Before Rio came into our lives, I took great pride in discovery, in finding new routes, sometimes to places so pristine I could swear no human had ever been. At first I was frustrated being with Rio, confined to an area within five miles of home. But because of what I learned by watching him respond to different signals in the land-scape, I began to feel a new, deeper relationship to place. I realized that what I was learning about place is actually very, very old.

The idea of place goes well beyond living there and getting to know everything about it. Being native might mean having generations of ancestors who have all lived in a place and given enough deep, old meaning to it to make it sacred.

Could I call the land I spent five years getting to know intimately "sacred"? Probably not in the Aboriginal sense. In this realm physical features have larger mean-ing to native people, meaning that has been passed down by stories and songs. Particular rocks and streams and mountain peaks have absorbed the songs and stories from hundreds of generations of people living in a specific landscape. If you are one of those people and you pass the rock or the river and you know the stories, you will feel the sacredness radiate out from that rock or river. Signals. If you know the stories.

The word *sacred* has different meanings, both per-sonally and culturally. My family considers sacred some of the early Mormon historical sites. The Sacred Grove, where Joseph Smith had his revolutionary vision that seeded the religion. Personally, I have places in mind—caves where I've camped, mountaintops, thin canyons with light bouncing between walls—where a mysterious combination of events penetrated deeply inside me, so much so that I think of those places as sacred. But the idea of sacredness is not something we moderns spend much time contemplating.

If it's possible to become native, how long does it take? Feeling a hint of what it means to be native was exhilarating at first, but then frustrating. Regardless of how much time I've spent in this landscape, as a white Euro-American, I'll always be a visitor.

If a place like Castle Valley throws out signals to me based on the briefest possible whiff of personal history, imagine the signals it would be sending out to the Native people whose history on this same land goes back a hundred generations. How much more information would I be getting from this landscape if I were native?

Then my train of thought collided head-on with another on the same track, and this hit me: The feelings I have about Castle Valley might pale when compared to those I'd have standing on the land where my ancestors were born, sniffing that same air, feeling the same breeze blowing against me that once blew against them. What new sense could I make? And I might learn something from my "homeland" about truly inhabiting a "place." I might remember how being "native" feels.

I had no choice. This idea overtook me like a fever. I knew if I was ever to truly understand the full capacity of place in my life, I needed to go to Europe and find the place I came from, where my ancestors were born and where they lived.

Like everyone I know, I grew up on stories told by grandparents about their grandparents and great-grandparents. The family stories I remembered were set in America. Being Caucasian, I knew I was Euro-American, and while I'd heard vague references to family in Canada, Wales, and England, I had nothing specific to go on. To know exactly where my ancestors came from, I first needed to know exactly who these people were.

That's where it got complicated.

Being a Mormon, I knew that finding my recent ancestors would be easy. I asked my father about my genealogy and had my pedigree chart in my hand within days. It looked a lot like the one the breeder gave us when we bought Rio. I'm perched on the left margin, between my mother's name and my father's. To the right of that, their parents, all four of my grandparents. I stopped there where my grandfather Williams appeared, just his name and dates. In my mind I saw him, cocking his head as he always did when he smiled, his thinning hair, in his office at his desk writing up orders with his perfect, antique handwriting. Below his name was Helen, my grandmother. Her picture bloomed, flooding my mind with memories, millions of them, especially of rare roast beef at Christmas and how the powder from the compact with the mirror in the lid made her cheeks smell and how I felt when she hugged me against her, her hat with the net over her eyes. The last column on the right had the names of all my great, great, great-grandparents, and I wondered about all their stories that I did not know.

I counted. Beginning with my grandparents, there were sixty ancestors on that chart, going back five generations to the early 1800s. As I scanned the list the first time, a few names popped out: James E. Talmage, my mother's father, a famous Mormon scholar and scientist and writer, who has books written about him and for whom college buildings are named. And Brigham Young, who led the Mormons across the country, who presided over the Church in its early days, who oversaw the building of Salt Lake City. Both men lived lives and performed deeds every child should know and emulate.

I noticed exotic names and places. Great, great, great-grandmothers, Tryphosia Shafter, Nabby Howe, and Delilah Emaline Andrus; and Uetikon (Switzerland), Bedford Leigh (England), and Monkeytown (Utah). There were so many that choosing one to follow back to a place, a source, would be a difficult endeavor.

I have thirty-two great, great, great-grandparents. Based on the little I knew about genetics, only 1/32 of my genetic material came from each of them. What would I understand about "place," about my homeland, if it was so spread out?

I had to start somewhere. To narrow my choices I set up three criteria: I would choose an ancestor who shared my surname, was born in Europe but died in America, and whom I'd never heard of before.

I quickly scanned the right column, filtering the names through the criteria I'd set up. The box in the top right-hand column jumped from the page.

```
WILLIAM WILLIAMS
B: 29 FEB 1808
SHREWSBURY, SHROPSHIRE, ENGLAND
D: 9 OCT 1863
CROSSING OF THE, SWEETWATER, WY
M: ABT 1825
SHREWSBURY, SHROPS., ENGL.
```

"Perfect," I thought. Not only was Williams this man's surname, but also his first name. I'd never heard of him. And he was born in England and died in Wyoming. "The Crossing of the Sweetwater" I wasn't sure about.

Don't ask me to explain why or how acknowledging that small box containing names and places and dates was the key to unlocking whatever door separated William Williams and me, the dead from the living, because I can't. But it did. It was as if he were out there wherever it is that dead people go, waiting for some signal that he was needed. Because that's what happened. He's stayed close to me ever since.

How else can I explain the nudges I feel just before I hear myself saying something I didn't know I knew? Or when I feel my point of view flex or switch, or when, in the middle of the night, a blinding insight hits me in the forehead like a laser beam, waking me up. Since discovering William Williams, I've noticed that all gray areas have disappeared from my life, leaving only black or white or vivid colors.

Immediately upon meeting William Williams, I felt a subtle but significant shift in my lifelong quest. Instead of exploring new and different ways to save the big wilderness, I began discovering how wilderness saves us. When moving forward in this direction I feel like clear water flowing. When I try moving in the wrong direction, William is very creative with the obstacles he throws in my way. If I continue in the wrong direction, I am metaphorically slammed down as if a rug has been pulled out from under me. Say William is real and the dead really are out there and active in another dimension, changed at death into another "phase" in the same way that heat changes water from liquid to vapor; if so, they must know things that are impossible for us to imagine, and they would love the chance to share what they know. Why would they care unless they knew that they had information that might help us? I've read that ghosts are people who died with unfinished business. Based on what I'm learning from William, collectively, all the dead have the unfinished business of seeing to it that the living stay focused on passing life onto the future.

The genealogical records were the beginning. I knew the place and time of William's birth and death. Two points on the long line that was this man's life—two simple points between which the unique story that is any man's life flows like a river, curving and falling, smooth and mirrorlike at one point, thundering through boulders at another. A bit more inquiry and I knew the names of his wife and children. And I learned that, unlike the other 951 souls with whom he sailed to America, he had not been baptized by Mormon missionaries.

The moment I began planning to visit Shrewsbury, England, his birthplace, I discovered that Charles Darwin was also born there, ten months after William. Since discovering Darwin in high school and then studying his life and work while pursuing my biology major in college, Darwin had been a hero of mine as an example of someone living a life of inquiry and imagination. William and Charles must have known each other.

When I traveled to Shrewsbury, I found that William was born in the poor Frankwell neighborhood, in a tiny house five minutes down a hill from The Mount, the mansion now known as the birthplace of Charles Darwin.

Later I learned that William and his family sailed to America on the *Cynosure* and crossed the plains with the Rosel Hyde Wagon Train. I now know he died not at "The Crossing of the Sweetwater" (the Mormon Trail crosses the Sweetwater River nine times in 120 miles) but at "Three Crossings of the Sweetwater," a specific point on the map. I've since camped there, waiting.

Although I've written about it, I don't know that Charles and William first met as ten-year-olds while playing at the Severn River. In fact, I don't know that they ever met at all. I imagine that they did.

I don't know that William's father built a stone wall for Dr. Darwin, Charles's father. I don't know that William became interested in nature's intricacies—particularly birds—because of Charles. I don't know that Charles and William stayed close when Charles left Shrewsbury to study, and when he left to travel the world on the *Beagle*. I know that William couldn't read or write, but I don't know that through friends, he followed Darwin's career—his thinking, his theories, the controversies he fueled, his personal dilemmas and his fame.

I don't know that whenever Charles Darwin visited Shrewsbury, he and William got together to talk about life, share ideas. I don't know that Charles Darwin's influence was a factor when, in 1857, William Williams chose not to be baptized a Mormon when his wife, Mary, and their children were. I don't know that he and Mary argued and fought about this, but I imagine that they did.

I don't know exactly why William and Mary and

their son, John George, waited another six years after those baptisms before leaving England for America, for Utah, the Mormon Promised Land.

I don't know if William hid in his belongings a copy of Darwin's books, *On the Origin of Species* and *The Voyage of the Beagle*, wrapped in a small British flag. I don't know that during the sea voyage to America, William had a young boy read passages to him. Or if William Williams memorized this one:

> As buds give rise by growth to fresh buds, and these,
> if vigorous, branch out and overtop on all sides many
> a feebler branch, so by generation I believe it has been
> with the great Tree of Life, which fills with its dead
> and broken branches the crust of the earth, and covers
> the surface with its ever branching and beautiful
> ramifications.

I don't know that William thought seriously about Darwin, the wonders of nature, and evolution while traveling from England to Utah, the wild world as his constant companion.

I don't know what exactly William Williams wants me to know. I don't know that being dead, he knows elemental truth. But I don't know that he doesn't.

Severn River, Shrewsbury, England

While thinking about William Williams—which I do often, whenever my mind is free—I fill in pieces of his story that were never written down and no one alive knows. His childhood, for example.

When young William was not gathering firewood to sell or hauling stone for his father who built walls for a living, he went to the river, his own world of wonder and magic, devoid of the hardships that haunted him daily. He would wander along the river, skipping stones or floating small wooden boats he'd built. Some days he fished with a perfect willow branch, with a worm impaled on a hook he'd found, hanging on a string.

I'm not sure his father was a stonemason, but there are stone walls everywhere—thousands of miles of walls, all built by hand. In my mind I saw William playing by the river in the same way that boys have always played beside rivers, the same way that I have played by rivers. I saw him drop his clothes and wade in the river eddies, challenging the back current by pushing his own weight against it. I saw his white body reflected in the river's green surface. I imagine William spending most of the little free time he had, alone. I could not imagine him slaving in the mines or in Mr. Marshall's textile mill with other children his age. The Industrial Revolution began a few years before William was born just miles downriver from Shrewsbury, where the first iron bridge was built across the Severn.

According to genealogical records, William's little brother, Samuel, was born on September 25, 1818. Who's to say that ten-year-old William didn't meet Charles Darwin then? When William sprinted out of his house that morning, he wasn't interested in exploring or fishing, he needed to be alone. The small house he lived in was always crowded, but that morning, the pain of his mother trying to give birth took up impossible space.

All night he had slept in short bursts, with deep moans coming from his dreams or the far side of his cramped house, he didn't know which. All night the walls seemed to glow from within as if they had absorbed the unfading lamplight. All night in the view from his bed he saw his father leaning over his mother, whose own shadow lurched in pain each time she moaned.

He got up at dawn and left after pulling on pants and a sweater that once belonged to his older brother. Outside, the clouds moved like a blanket being pulled across the sky, revealing the brightest stars and a fading, crescent moon, and then the thickening yellow line preceding the rising sun.

As William ran past the flat stones his father had stacked next to the house and past the hammers soaking in the wooden bucket to keep their heads tight, he saw Dr. Darwin stepping down from his carriage. His carriage had only one seat, and all the boys in the neighborhood were sure it was because the poor horse had a difficult enough time pulling Dr. Robert's mass—twenty stone, or nearly 300 pounds. Moisture steamed off the back of that black horse.

William ran down the small lane, stretching his face to break open the mask sleep had left, letting in the fall air. Houses like his lined the road, all of them lit and busy. Dogs barked, doors opened and closed as women who looked older than their age left to gather firewood and big-headed men hurried to fields or factories. "Any news?" he heard his neighbors ask as he passed them on the street. William shook his head no. A few hungry children and sheep and the man selling lamp oil accounted for the other morning sounds.

Although his father had not mentioned it, William knew that this baby was having difficulty entering the world. Otherwise, why send for Dr. Robert?

William ran down the road, cut to the alley behind the blacksmith shop, and slid down the bank to the river. It had been raining lightly and he stopped to lean against a flat rock warmed by the one beam of sun that had managed to burn through the clouds. While looking down at the warm mud bubbling up through his toes and thinking how mud might be the truest, most real thing he knew, he noticed the track of a large bird, which he could not fully cover with his outspread hand. Two feet away was another, and another beyond that, sinking deeper as the mud softened where the river bent. With the hope of seeing the bird but also wanting to keep from sinking in the mud, William ducked into a small tunnel made by rushes bending against the vertical bank cut by a recent flood. William found the tracks on the other side, where they were paralleled by more tracks, those of a boy about his size, a boy wearing shoes.

William's attention to the tracks worked to obliterate from his mind the pain back at his house and to silence the memory of his mother's sounds. He took two steps toward the river and stood straight up. In front of him, crouched behind a wooden tangle, was the boy the tracks belonged to, motioning for William to join him.

It was young Charles Darwin. Charles frequently accompanied his father on house calls. Not knowing how long this birth might take, Dr. Robert had sent his son to the river. This was not a hardship. Since his own mother's death the year before, young Charles often retreated to the river.

Charles whispered something William could not hear.

"Pardon?" William said.

The boy whispered louder. "Over there. Quiet."

William rose slowly to see above the blind. Across the river a tall gray bird moved slowly into view, its yellow beak aimed down toward the river. The two boys watched silently until the bird stood up straight, took three hard wingbeats, and was airborne down the river.

"It is a sacred stork from a magic country," the boy said. "It may have just delivered your mother's baby."

William looked hard for clues on the boy's face as to whether he believed what he was saying. William didn't know it at the time, but that was not the last thing Charles Darwin would say that would make him wonder about the confusing differences between knowledge, memory, and imagination.

William was eager to show Charles a place he knew where the river was quiet and, when the light was just right, an abandoned trunk could be seen lying on the bottom.

Charles said, "Very well. Let's go." Then, "I've found three new feathers, four interesting pebbles, and a smooth piece of glass." He paused. "I have numerous collections."

Charles was silent during the five-minute walk along the river. At first William thought Charles was conceited, having no desire to talk with someone as poor as he was. William realized later that it was not conceit that made Charles quiet but that he hated distraction. By the time they reached the river, Charles had pocketed two more perfect pebbles and one feather (gray with a bright blue top edge, possibly a jay), stopped to touch three different plants, and looked at one set of animal tracks in the mud. William thought they were those of a small dog. Charles said, "Fox."

Charles was a thick boy with a big nose and curly brown hair. He was wearing knickers and a white shirt, clothes that had they been owned by William would have been worn only to church. He had gray, dreamy eyes that reflected the sky.

By contrast, William had a broad chest and was tall for a ten-year-old. He had blond hair closer to white, and his mother often commented that his blue eyes were the only color on gray, winter days. His hands were thick and cracked from hard work, and his legs were as hard as wood from walking and running. William could count the times he had been in a carriage during his life. Four.

Rain began to fall.

William might've gone home, but his young ego would rather have had Charles be the one to choose dry comfort over a walk by the river. But Charles didn't seem to notice the rain.

At the edge of the river, Charles paused, then sunk quietly to his haunches and stared out across the water, dimpled by halfpenny-sized raindrops hitting the surface. Birds floated in the eddy on the far side.

"Ducks," William said.

"Mallards," said Charles.

William noticed the dampness from the rain soaking through his sweater. He followed Charles along the riverbank and then back behind a thick grouping of willows, which had bent back, forming what two young boys might see as a fort. Rain dripped from the back of Charles's hair. Charles squatted down.

"We can watch from here," he said.

Watch what? William thought.

They sat there until William's legs grew stiff and the willow roof did not protect them from the water that they were beginning to breathe in through their noses. Charles rotated his head left, then right, then back. Nothing happened. Nothing moved but the river and the rain.

The walk back was quicker until Charles noticed a beetle moving to the left of the path. He stooped, picked it up, and held it firmly between his thumb and forefinger, its front legs slowly pawing the air. He held it close as if he were looking in its eye, then released it, letting it crawl across his hand. He inspected it for every detail, rotating his hand one way and then the other.

"The colors on his back change," he said.

William moved closer and watched the light change the color of the beetle's back from black to iridescent green.

"Why?" William asked.

"There's a good reason," he said. "I just don't know what it is." For some reason the reply sounded religious to William, but he sensed that Charles hadn't intended it that way. Charles stooped again, nudged the beetle off his arm onto the ground and into the protection of a low bush. William could think only of the dozens of beetles just like that he had smashed with his boot.

They hurried back to the house. The carriage hadn't moved. Charles reached in under the seat and retrieved a leather case with a shoulder strap. He unbuckled the flap and from inside pulled two small, brown books.

"Natural history," he said. "My father just gave them to me. They belonged to my uncle."

Charles put one book back in the case and began turning through the pages of the other, *Insects*, by Brooks, 1763. He ran his finger over a page and stopped.

"Here," he said. "Have a look."

William would remember that moment because the book was the first he'd ever held that was not a Bible. In front of him on a page covered with engravings of different beetles was the exact likeness of the one they had seen crossing the path from the river.

A hinge squeaked as the door to the house opened. Dr. Robert came out looking tired, but he was smiling. His bag was in one hand, and he put his hat on with the other. John, William's father, stood behind him with one hand on Dr. Robert's shoulder. He seemed very happy. They both seemed very happy. From inside William could hear the first hungry cries of his new brother, Samuel.

"About your fee—" William's father started to ask.

"We will work it out," said Dr. Robert. "I'll need a wall moved to accommodate a new garden I've planned for spring."

William watched Dr. Robert and Charles ride off in the carriage. Charles looked back and William waved.

He thought he saw Charles smile. William tried to recall Charles smiling during their walk to the river, but he couldn't.

William's family had no more babies, and Charles got sent off to boarding school. Although they didn't see each other over the next few years, the influence Charles had over William was apparent around William's house. He nailed a board to the windowsill where birds could find crumbs he left for them. And he'd convinced his mother that spiders were important for the insects they ate, and she left the webs they built inside their house. William followed to their sources the sounds he'd always heard along the river—squirrels, insects rubbing their wings or legs against one another, small innocent birds. On clear nights he went to the river, the darkest place he knew, and drew stars in their positions with a stick in the hard sand and wondered about the spaces between them. He connected the stars with lines, making his own constellations. It was years before he discovered he was not the first to do this. In those rare moments when his mind was quiet, thoughts seemed to bounce between different parts of his brain. William admitted that he was envious of Charles and the time he had to roam the countryside and explore the riverbank. He wished to learn the correct name for things, to go to school. But then William's father said he should be proud of the walls they'd built together, and William was.

The last part of the story, William's fascination with nature and his desire to learn, surprised me. Each word seemed to materialize like heat or light in my mind the moment before I typed it, the result of fueling my imagination with the facts I'd found. In William's case, my imagination had created a lot from a little. What I failed to realize until I reread the story was that yes, the story was the combination of fact and imagination but that the line between them had blurred. The constellations, the bird feeders, the spiders, and the desire for time to wander came, not from my imagination, but from my life. I'd shifted between memory and imagination without being aware of it. Since William and I are related, I questioned whether shifting details between individuals in different generations really matters. This is a story, I remembered, and although we're seldom aware of it, stories find us.

THREE

Solitude Wash, Book Cliffs, Utah

Looking back, the decade after discovering William Williams was laced with moments involving key decisions around work or professional projects, significant personal interactions, and surprising impressions. During these instances I felt what I now believe was William's hand on my shoulder as he guided me inward toward a dimension of knowledge which I was beginning to trust. I realize now that I was being signaled to respond from my deepest, truest self, rather than from the modern surface of my life that seeks approval and acceptance. I benefited when I paid attention to those signals and suffered when I didn't.

Although I grew comfortable moving between worlds, I wasn't good at articulating it. Plus, if I'm being honest, what I knew embarrassed me. Knowing my inner world was as rich and beautiful but with more dimensions than my outer world did not give me the confidence I needed to talk about it. I also felt external pressure. The wilderness I loved was subjected to growing threats from the motorized recreationists, and more seriously from the energy industry as it capitalized on America's redoubled commitment to reducing its dependence on foreign oil. And mounting evidence indicated that if the world didn't begin weaning itself from carbon, global climate change would leave our children facing an unrecognizable and desperate future. Even if political will focused entirely on solving this problem, truly viable solutions didn't seem to exist. I knew that the wilderness saves us. I needed to figure out how, and get on it.

When the call came from Scott Groene, the executive director for the Southern Utah Wilderness Alliance, asking me to consider working as a field advocate, my inner world lit up. SUWA, a gutsy band of wilderness warriors responsible for holding the line on wilderness, fighting back dozens of attacks from a slew of conservative politicians going back to the mid-1980s, was embarking on a new campaign. Part of my job would be working with different rural county officials to whom wilderness is a curse, a desecration of all they believed in or thought they'd been promised. They were ready, once and for all, to hold their noses and get Wilderness legislation passed. They wanted to be done with it forever. Naïvely I saw this as a platform for exploring and experimenting with my theory. If wilderness can "save us," could I convince its most ardent detractors? I was skeptical. Secondarily, I would conduct fieldwork. SUWA has always committed considerable effort to knowing more about the landscape than even the Bureau of Land Management, under whose jurisdiction it falls. In particular, having on-the-ground knowledge of the roads is key, as Wilderness, by definition, has no roads. My job would be to visit the more remote areas being recommended for Wilderness designation to determine whether lines on the map were in fact roads or trails, or the result of seismic measurements or impassibly ancient mining exploration, or if they even existed at all. If I found an actual "road" in a potential Wilderness unit, I needed to walk it to document if it did actually provide access to a stock tank, mine, scenic viewpoint, or something historic. I would take photos and make notes.

Within months of starting, my work with the County Wilderness campaign slowed to a crawl when we realized that the real work was being done in meetings to which we were not invited. Not once in all the meetings we were invited to did I find the space to discuss ideas, as everyone seemed to have made up their minds long before. My fieldwork, however, quickly became invaluable in my own process to understand just what is going on in the world. Many, many long, quiet days immersed in wildness inspired me and stoked my imagination.

A particular day in the Book Cliffs was typical in some ways, unique in others.

We'd started early that morning, Rio and me, and of course William Williams, who never seems too far away. An early spring warm spell was the excuse I needed to continue the work I'd started the previous fall, documenting a few confusing routes in the Book Cliffs, north of Moab.

A recent flood had deposited a wall of rocks blocking the third Solitude Wash crossing. And according to my map, we still had miles to go before reaching the Bench Road, a primitive, eighty-mile-long two-track marking the southern boundary of the Book Cliff's four Wilderness Study Areas. I got out, hoping to find an alternative to turning back the way we'd come. If I moved a few rocks and did some strategic shoveling and some careful driving, Ford would likely get through. First, I thought, I'll walk upstream a ways to look around the next corner while I loosen up.

Driving between Salt Lake City and our home in Castle Valley, I have often wondered about the Book Cliffs—the massive, castlelike formation running parallel to I-70, spreading west from Colorado to Highway 6, which heads north from Green River to Price, Utah. I'd heard about the wild country to be found in the Book Cliffs but that no one really goes there. Until recently the Book Cliffs have been that great unknown off to the north, so massive and long and austere, nearly cutting the state in half. No one I knew ever really explored or seemed to care much about the Book Cliffs. The word *daunting* comes to mind when I think of the Book Cliffs. No hope of rescue. There be dragons. Pure wilderness.

After driving for two hours, walking felt good. The same flash flood that blocked the road where we left

Ford had cleansed the creek bed of its entire past—all its weather and sound and any hint of green. I felt, in that sharp air and deep orange light, that I too had been reborn.

Although the landscape on both sides of the road seemed wild, the deep pink color on my map showed only the landscape to my right as having "wilderness character"—a recent classification resulting from how complicated federal land designation has become. The map showed a heavy black line representing the washed-out road I walked along as the Wilderness boundary.

Rio was out on patrol, assessing any potential danger. What was left of the flood flowed clear, an inch-deep and never too wide to step across. The creek bottom was dense, moist sand, my footsteps leaving only vague tracks. Rocks the flood left behind were small, able to duck the crush of water that the big boulders had not. Ahead, a clear route was visible and I turned back to get the truck. I would be able to drive at least a mile and, at most, all the way to Green River.

"Rio, this way," I yelled, knowing he was close.

Back leaning against Ford, I surveyed the situation, which seemed more complicated than before. I was ready to forget the project, turn around, and move onto a different area when, suddenly, a large ghost rock absorbed all my attention. I chuckled to myself, knowing that William Williams must be nearby. Suddenly a path appeared through the morass. Tilting up the large white rock and moving four more manageable rocks to the side would create a large and smooth enough space to drive between the three others I knew could not be budged.

That white stone was oblong and flat on one end. I picked up the other end, tilting it upright. As if some primitive power or force, or even time itself, that had been trapped beneath it suddenly escaped, air gusted by me, thick and moist and charged with presence. I rocked the tall stone back and forth until it stood on its own.

Rocks and stones are different. I first realized this years ago in England while looking for clues to William's life. Rocks are untouched by humans. Stones, in contrast, have been moved, carved, stacked, turned, thrown—by humans. This is not complicated. During a darker part of our history, people thought to be witches were not "rocked" but "stoned." An old London street is made of cobblestones, never cobble rocks. If you're lucky, you've been to an ocean location having not a "stony" but "rocky" coastline.

As if due to some genetically induced propensity that has something to do with why I imagined William's father to be a stonemason, I love to move and stack rocks. I love the concentration it requires, knowing that there is always a place on one rock that allows it to stand firmly on the one beneath it. Flat ones are easy, and my record on a beach in Maine is twelve high. I've turned entire beaches—on the Canning River in the Arctic, Cataract Canyon in southern Utah, Acadia National Park—into sculpture galleries. I like the temporary nature of my creations, knowing that with the next high water or big wind, the stones I've stacked will fall and quickly disappear into randomness where I found them. In a public place, I'll take down my sculptures when I'm finished, not wanting them to distract the next visitor.

There are places near our home where I go regularly to stack rocks as if part of a mysterious therapy. Years ago, a flash flood left a dozen different-sized boulders at the north end of our driveway that now serve as the base for the many stacks that we use as the landmark for finding our way home. Weekly, I stack rocks for hours at the edge of the Colorado where a side stream entering that river deposits perfect specimens. When I'm completely focused on my task, the rocks I'm to use seem to stand out among the others. Many of those rocks are heavy, and when I'm moving them I think back to England and particularly Stonehenge, built with stones, some weighing five tons and moved over two hundred miles by Neolithic workers.

John Berger writes, "Perhaps the proverbial nature of the stone changed when prehistory became history. . . . To place a stone upright so that it stands vertical is an act of symbolic recognition; the stone becomes a presence; a dialogue begins." He was echoing what others had writ- ten, that revealing a stone's full presence and meaning by turning it up made our first ancestors fully human. That prehistoric stones, untouched, untilted, had no meaning or mystery until our ancestors moved and placed them.

If turning a stone upright marked the transition

from prehistory to history, stripping stones of their meaning and symbolism may mark our latest transition to modernity. Lately they're usually seen only as obstacles or for their potential as a building material. Turning up that stone that day in Solitude Wash now seems an act of both modernity—I needed to move it to continue on in my truck—and history—I felt something released from beneath it as I tilted it up. The dual nature of that stone suggests that time may be more than a line with a beginning and an end. But cyclical, circular, or even better, in a spiral, *spiralical*—around but also upward, onward toward something barely possible and yet to be imagined.

During the dawn of civilization our first farmer-ancestors prepared those first planting fields by moving the rocks originally deposited there by glaciers, exploding volcanoes, or ancient rivers. Depending on a stone's weight, there is a maximum distance one wants to carry it. Building walls was the most efficient way to store rocks cleared from early fields. And, as what may have been an unintended consequence, those first walls marked property. *Since this linear pile of rocks divides this space where we're learning to grow plants, that side must be yours and this side mine. Right?* We know what happened from there. *My crops are more robust than yours. Therefore, you must stay on your side of the wall. But why is your space bigger than mine? And don't ever come on my side of the wall.* And so on.

Did those early gardeners feel that same release as

they picked up those first rocks—that same equalizing, flowing between that dark and ancient world and the new, forever different one? I don't think so. Those rocks were nothing but a nuisance.

Moving stones opens a passage between worlds. Old time mixes with new, balances the mystery. That is what I felt that day in Solitude Wash. Moving rocks is different. Moving rocks can be a necessary pain in the ass.

We've separated ourselves from the reservoir of our own deepest past, isolating us from our complete history. I imagine before cement, before pavement, the past and present mixing freely, all of us living in the present, one point in the infinite flow of time. Trapped now, the past builds up beneath us, pressurized.

Tilting up that stone in Solitude Wash released that pressure. I felt it—not wind, not light, neither unfamiliar nor familiar. Beyond familiar in substance and flow and force—magnetism or gravity but not quite. I saw time, not as measurement or scale but as a force. Time became movement. My own oldest cells came alive—my mammalian, reptilian cells, my bacterial cells—activated by that swampy sweet smell riding on a breeze having just passed over something that has been buried for a long, long time.

I sensed that what came up from beneath that rock, that *stone*, was dangerous to everything we've bet on.

I moved four more large stones to the edge of the original road. Then I threw a dozen smaller stones to the side and moved three flatter ones to level out the route I planned for Ford's tires.

The sun was high overhead by the time Rio jumped into the cab and I followed. Small sun-warmed flies, diamond silhouettes in the blazing sun, buzzed around, grabbed one at a time by a large metallic-green dragonfly. Rio drank from the bowl that fit perfectly into the coffee cup holder on Ford's console. I pulled the lever shifting into four-wheel drive, low range—something I'd done only a dozen times in the quarter-million miles I'd driven that truck.

I barely released the clutch and Ford lurched, then launched. I love torque. I love the word and I love the force. Ford came alive, as if pulled along by a team of huge oxen that knew exactly where to go. As we crawled steadily through the passage I'd created, I marveled how close I'd come to missing what William Williams knew I needed to know.

Without once nicking its skid plate, Ford dropped back into the creek. Shifting gears, we moved steadily upstream, passing first the line cabin, the farthest point to which we'd walked earlier, and then an old corral we'd missed. We followed the original route as it cut across the spaces formed by large bends in the creek. In and out of the creek, we went for one mile, for two.

The canyon walls closed in and our movement slowed and became more methodical, like thickening blood moving through a long, twisting vein. On smooth, hard sand

and the small but flat, evenly spaced rocks, we pulsed up that creek.

It all ended where the high-speed flood had gashed a wall into the wash of sand and rock and logs the diameter of small melons, and dropped the creek bed five vertical feet. I got out to survey the obstacle and marvel at the power of water.

I sat down, back to a large boulder to look at the map. Ten miles short of my goal, we'd have to turn back.

The power released by that first stone was still with me, and I thought about England, where I'd spent six weeks getting to know William, but also following guidebooks to places where stones were moved and placed upright and stacked—one perfectly upon another and another. I read many books speculating on why people did this thousands of years ago. And others about stone as an archetype, across all time and all place: a universal symbol of power, steadfastness, sexuality, eternity, endurance. All that but, most importantly, for our own deepest, most elemental and resilient self.

We've lost all context for this. Have we consciously abandoned the meaning of stone? Without context there is only mystery.

To many, there is neither context nor mystery, only disdain for a people who might still believe in something as simple as the meaning to be gained from a stone. Modern religion believes it has silenced the stones. In many cases the eighteenth-century English church destroyed important but threatening cultural sites of massive standing stones, burial quoits, and menhirs, eliminating the possibility that the stones might be speaking. The modern world cannot afford to have anyone listening to stones.

Without those stories, those stones would be rocks. A stone, then, is a rock with a story.

I backed up carefully down the tight, rock-strewn wash. After thirty yards, the canyon opened. After a six-point turnaround, some serious clutch work, and an over-revved engine, we were facing back the way we came.

I followed the path I'd made back through the obstacle without slowing down, our speed rarely registered on the speedometer anyway, stopping once we'd cleared it. The long, pale pink rock I'd tilted upward stood tall among the others. I could wrestle it into the back of Ford and take it home. It might look good standing upright on our porch. No. Seeing the place the flood left it still engraved in the sandy surface, I laid it back exactly how I'd found it. High above, wind pulled clouds apart as if they were made of cotton.

The silence thickened and settled once Ford stopped and I shut down the engine. The sound of that flood must have been deafening—thousands of tumbling boulders banging against one another, millions of gallons of water flushing and scouring. These canyons have not been carved gradually, I thought.

It's late now. I'm almost home, tired physically, but the solitude I've breathed in all day, eaten like food, keeps me alert and hopeful. Sweet dessert. Here, everything turns wild at night. A fox or deer or coyote could cross the road. An owl might lift its mouse meal from the shoulder. Not one car this time of year. I imagine the cliff mass on the right and on the left, below, the immortal river with its permanent boulders, each its own planet. Night-sounding canyons. The dark universe explodes in size and detail, compressing the glow from Ford's headlights as they drill and carve and struggle to overcome it. I shift down and Ford climbs the road through the Moenkopi hills, the portal, and follows its twisting route toward the pass. Lights dot Castle Valley below me, tucked and safe between vast wilderness to the east and west. The moonless air is dark, but our giant guardian cottonwood—the second biggest on earth, I hear—stands silhouetted black against it, its huge mass absorbing last light remnants.

I pass the dark cemetery. Standing and stacked stones mark graves there. Cemeteries—the one place we still allow stones their meaning.

I turn on the fourth road past the cemetery. Between rut and rock Ford's headlights find the only smooth line. I pass the tall fence on the left keeping deer out of the vineyard, then the neighbor's numbered boulder on the right. I slow down when a dozen deer rise in the sage—green laserlike eye shine, then night-blurred, ghostlike bodies. Moving away slowly, they're bothered, not scared. Ahead, high-beam light finds stacked stones prodding and probing the darkness, looming, marking our driveway. Even asleep, Rio knows we're home, unfurls, perches against the dash. My hands relax on the steering wheel. Ford can take it from here. Recent wind has knocked many smaller stones from my careful statues now needing repair.

We park in front of our house. Rio jumps out, stretches, sniffs the air, pees onto a rabbitbrush. When I turn it counterclockwise to "off," the headlight knob detonates a massive explosion with the new darkness, painting the sky with stars.

The next morning and gray light fills our room. Then yellow. Then orange. I find shorts and shoes and a warm shirt, and Rio does his downward dog in a sun puddle just his size. We're out through the back door for our morning ritual, the spring air a clear shock. We'll go due south, turning east and over the fence separating our private land from public. On a deer path we'll follow the fence north to the road, to the driveway, back home. Full circle.

Between yucca and sage we stop on the long dike, the length of a soccer field, built to catch floods coming out of the southern mountains. Silted in on the south, its north face is a tilted wall of skull-sized rocks, bleached by the sun. Crossing the wash, the floods carve deeper each time they come. We climb the barbed-wire fence and follow a wall built of dry white rocks—I can't say why. Distant coyotes howl and yap, unusual in the morning.

The adjacent property, now covered in cheatgrass and thistle, is nearly void of rocks. I think back to Solitude Wash, the thoughts I had there, that stone I uprighted. I've been across this field a hundred times but never thought about how flat and smooth it is. Today I'm sure that hay was once raised here. To do that they moved the stones, stacked them into walls. Built that dike. Of course.

The path passes rusted pipes, an old pump motor, then intersects the road. Neighbor dogs bark and exotic game hens clatter and cluck and warn as we pass.

Prehistory is infinite. Darwin connected us genealogically, not only back through larger and larger branches of the tree of life to its very trunk, but down to its roots and out to that steamy swamp where life began with perfectly combined elements from some long-time-ago and very faraway exploding star. Today there's no beginning we can find, which renders it infinite. I want to incorporate, absorb some of that prehistory into my own personal history. Imagining what difference that might make obliterates everything as I walk toward the driveway, the growing warmth, sun height, greening cottonwoods, the shadow bleeding down from the cliff boundary of the Mary Jane Canyon Wilderness.

If the nature of stones changed when prehistory became history—when a major transition of time occurred—it did again when history became modernity.

Then, I hear William's voice in my head. "Could the opposite be true?"

Perhaps, instead of waiting for time epochs to shift, which has traditionally changed the "nature of stones," we consciously tilt up or aesthetically stack those once moved to make room for growing hay, for building dikes to fend off destructive floods, building walls—and in doing so reestablish their presence and meaning. What if this conscious gesture could help us move forward beyond modernity in time to avoid any irrevocable damage to our species or our planet? Modernity has actually diminished our "humanness," according to evolution's trajectory, by dooming our future. By acknowledging a stone's full and ancient power we might once again become "fully human."

At the driveway entrance, we've got time, I think, stopping. I'll add stones to my cairns, from which many have fallen.

Many of those lying on the ground nearby are flat and easily stacked. The others, the round ones, require focus and my softest touch. These rocks were prehistoric when they lay randomly in that wild landscape. Ranch workers moving them into walls, into that dike, clearing the field to grow hay was not historic, and those men did not become more fully human but modern. I imagine that before, when archaic hunters stepped between those stones while looking for game, they imbued them with meaning and mystery and, therefore, history. Unchanged in substance and form and weight and color, those stones carry different contexts through time.

Now, by stacking them, I give them a new story, not their first story of being popped from the high wall by expanding ice on a frigid night, then swept into and tumbled by water into shape. A rock, then, is a stone that has not yet been given a story. It has a story, just not our story. Prehistory may become history once we add our story.

The flood-dropped boulders form a corner at our driveway entrance. The largest lies at the point, atop which a large, oblong stone points upright. In the three years since I placed it there, no wind has had the strength to tip or move or make it fall. From the storm-scattered stones beneath it, I select the nearly perfect egglike stone—a foot long, chipped on one end. That chip, I think, might allow it to stand on top of the high, oblong stone on the corner boulder.

Holding the egg in both hands—it must weigh fifteen pounds—I pivot it on the point where its chipped end meets the tall stone below it, first clockwise in circles of decreasing diameter. Then counterclockwise, feeling for that tiny but solid point where the two surfaces match. Smaller and smaller circles, feeling that small solid point at each rotation, stopping briefly, relaxing my grip, checking for balance. Then back and forth, slightly—the top moving a centimeter, then less, then less. Checking. The egg, standing nearly on its own as if embraced by a magic and dense force field forming between it and my curved hands. It falls a distance I can feel but not see. I take a deep breath, then another. My neck muscles strain, my forearms throb from stone isometrics. I sweat. I finally feel that flat, shared surface expand. As if both surfaces mysteriously change, evolve to accommodate each other.

The eggstone stands firm. I move my hands out from it an inch, then three. Then I move back and against the backdrop of Castleton Tower, I watch this new creation—very beautiful, very temporary.

FOUR

Aboard the Cynosure, *Atlantic Ocean*

Early in my research, I discovered the *Cynosure*, the packet ship that carried William, his wife and youngest son, and 951 other Saints from England to America. I know that the ship left Liverpool on May 30, 1863, and arrived in New York on July 19, a total of fifty days at sea. From the journal of David Stuart, who was set apart as the Mormon leader of the group, I learned that he divided the immigrants into six wards, each with its own leader and its own chorus, and that concerts were held at every opportunity. Seven babies were born during the crossing, and seven couples were married. I know the captain lost his bearings and for days afterward the ship tossed about in the fog. And when the fog finally lifted, the ship was surrounded by fourteen icebergs.

I imagine William standing on deck alone, staring down into the cold fog as the *Cynosure*, its sails down, tilted and bounced on the rough surface of the sea. A dark bird with white wing patches floated nearly motionless below, on the surface of the green ocean. Suddenly

Ledger from the *Cynosure*—"Wm Williams, Mary, and John" near the bottom.

William was back from his thoughts, which, like lead boots, pulled him into the depths, memory by memory. With the fog thickness and long days that time of year— June had become July—he wasn't sure which missed meal caused his hunger pangs.

For days, the *Cynosure* had bobbed in the waves, the air eerily silent. That the captain had lost his way in the fog was the latest rumor, which managed to circulate freely below deck where fresh air could not.

Moments after coming on deck, having once again been overcome by the mixed stench of the vomit of the seasick, hundreds of unclean bodies, and wet wool, he wondered about the color and clarity of seawater: Why was it opaque? What color would it be in a small glass? Darwin had planted this small seed of inquiry, in this case, with a few paragraphs in *Voyage*. William referred to Darwin's book, *The Voyage of the Beagle*, as "*Voyage*" and to *On the Origin of Species*, the other book Darwin had given him, as simply "*Origin*." The evening before, as he did almost daily, William signaled young Jonathan during the singing of hymns that seemed to go on—and on and on—constantly, and the two of them snuck away to a quiet and well-lit corner of the deck. On overturned wooden boxes they sat, Jonathan reading to William random sections of either of Darwin's books and sometimes both. Looking down into the dark sea from the fog-curtained deck, William recalled from a recent reading Darwin's description of reddish-tinted water he had dipped from—where was it—somewhere off the coast of Chile and examined under a microscope. As they often did, Darwin's words fueled William's imagination. While Jonathan read, William watched in his mind's eye a swarm of tiny oval beings darting about, powered by a million vibrating hairs, which expanded then exploded into a brownish ooze, giving its color to the water. Were there, he wondered, similar organisms here in the far north exploding invisibly, turning the water below him green? He would need a microscope to know.

He'd love to have his own microscope. Would he be able to buy a microscope in Utah he wondered as his thoughts dipped further into the darkness. Certainly not. In America? Realistically, anything beautiful or of a sophisticated nature, anything other than the most basic necessities, would likely come from England. How much would that cost?

How would he find work in Utah? Trained as a joiner in a furniture plant, would his skill have value in Utah? How long would getting settled take? Would the money he borrowed from the Emigration Fund last? These were his questions, strung together like beads.

He redid familiar calculations: the seven pounds they got selling everything they could not carry plus the thirty (ten for each of them) they borrowed minus twelve six for the ocean passage (four eight each for he and Mary; three for John George, not yet an adult) leaves twenty-four four and then the three for new necessities leaving twenty-one four. He figured ten for the two months getting through the wilderness would take, hoping that included the boat and the train to the place they called Florence, Nebraska, where the real journey would begin. Would they leave right away? What if they stayed a while in Florence? What would that cost?

William found these thoughts and calculations had worn deep pathways in his brain. Although he'd been over the numbers—he couldn't read but he did learn to add and subtract during the years he spent at his furniture job—a hundred times, they always came out the same.

Not aware of how long he'd been staring into the

dark green water below him, or the depth to which his gaze had penetrated, William thought back to that moment in their house—the missionaries with the papers to sign in exchange for the loan to make the journey. His last excuse—"We simply cannot afford to destroy this stable life and travel to America"—was no longer valid. Mary signed first and didn't smile as she pushed the papers across the table toward him.

While his signature was his agreement to pay back the thirty pounds they were borrowing, it was also his surrender. He hoped his signing would heal the gash religion had slowly cut away from the bond between him and Mary, because this was the only reason that mattered. It was the beginning, he thought, but the healing always takes longer than the cutting.

I imagined William's thoughts taking him back to the day the missionaries first came. He and Mary pulling the few chairs they owned around the table—the table that was used for everything from sewing and washing clothes to eating. William chose the broken chair because he knew how to sit in it without falling. Since all the houses were built in back-to-back rows divided by a common wall, a neighbor baby could be heard crying, along with hungry dogs and the buzz and drone of the many struggles. The familiar smell from the combined smoke of a dozen street-side cooking fires wafted through the open window.

Nineteenth-century Mormon missionaries in Europe were responsible for converting individuals and families to the faith and then arranging their emigration to Utah.

As the missionaries told the Mormon story about Joseph Smith's vision of Christ in America after his resurrection, about the newly settled Eden, about everlasting life, William looked around at the worn coats and clothes, mended dozens of times, hanging from hooks on the walls, then over at the one large kettle and two small pans that, along with his aging tools, accounted for what he owned in the world.

He recalled something shifting inside him when missionaries mentioned America, the City of the Saints, a place called Salt Lake City, in Utah, in America's western wilderness frontier, where anything was possible. Did a small spark light up in the back of his brain? Did a fully formed multicolored dream form in his mind? Or did one simple blood-red drop of dense liquid fall into the dirty gray water his life had become, exploding, giving everything around him a new color? Wasn't he too old and settled to start over?

William put the Mormon story in context with other religious stories, including those he had heard since his youth at St. Chad's Cathedral on those Sundays with his mother when he didn't sneak out to play. His concern grew when the conversation switched to Utah and Mary's eyes widened.

Developing a Mormon culture in Utah required bodies.

Missionaries knew that regardless of how one felt about Mormonism, the chance to go to America for a new start and unlimited opportunity was a major incentive for many converts.

In my mind, Mary was the practical one. She stretched over incredible distances the meager money William earned at his factory job. She was a great cook who could sew and fix anything. She taught their children to read and write and do simple arithmetic. William taught them to identify the wild plants and animals living on Shrewsbury's fringes. William taught them to wonder and to think and ask questions—even those that could not be answered. Mary's eyes widened when she heard the opportunity the missionaries spoke of. She'd read about America and its promise, but until meeting the Mormon missionaries, she never imagined living there.

William wondered why people are so willing to discount their own beliefs but open wide to a story told by someone they couldn't know or trust because he was dead, about a people living in another time and place. He thought hard to connect the religious implications of Mormonism with anything he knew from his own experience.

Mary accepted the challenge from the missionaries to read the Book of Mormon and fast and pray for answers about its truthfulness. The spirit may have "struck" her as it did their oldest son, my great, great-grandfather, Thomas Valentine Williams, nine years before. But perhaps at age forty-four she realized that joining the Mormon Church offered her family a ticket to America and the one chance to climb out of their dim circumstance.

Although nothing is known about the marriage of William and Mary Williams, I hear through time's thick walls the tone and intensity of the conversations that took place between 1852, when Mary and their children were baptized and William wasn't, and 1863, when they left for America with their youngest son, John George.

I know that in those eleven years Mary and William went around and around on this one. I imagine that during that period William spent much more time alone in his shop, hoping to avoid one more "little chat" with Mary—that they argued more then than in the first twenty-two years of their marriage. Or with his friends at the pub, or just "out," wandering along the Severn River as it passed through Shrewsbury.

Although those close to him wondered, no one knew if William's dramatically increased interest in birds had anything to do with that first visit from the Mormon missionaries. Shortly afterward he started vaporizing in the morning from the crowded bed he shared with Mary, or almost invisibly from the dinner table at night. He would be found, if he was found at all, beneath the awning he had built to convert the back of the house into a simple workshop, bending willows around the wooden frames to create bird feeders of his own unique design.

One particular morning, as he had done nearly every morning in recent years, William, with a cup of steaming tea, stood back from the house where he could see each of the feeders he had placed atop tall poles sunk into the hard ground. He noticed that rather than the random mix of birds he'd grown used to finding feeding there (house sparrows, martins, swallows), starlings had crowded into each of his twelve feeders, their black feathers glowing luminescent in the first sun.

He would be taking a rare day off.

William went back into the house for his hat and the pail filled with his midday dinner—old bread and a canister of watery soup in which to soak it. Mary bustled about as was her nature, getting the youngest off to his job in the nearby mill. Other than the perfunctory, William and Mary didn't speak that morning, which wasn't unusual. He didn't tell her that instead of work, he would walk to Mitchell's Cove and sit with his dead ancestors against the ancient stones standing there. Of course he didn't.

He did tell her he would miss supper.

Since her own baptism, Mary had been pushing William to join the Mormons and take his family to America, to Utah. William, consciously or not, had found new ways to fill the limited free time he had between work at the furniture factory and sleep. Mary knew that his birds and his walks, plus the one additional evening he spent with friends in the pub, were all an effort to avoid discussing Mormons and America, subjects on which they had long ago reached an impasse.

Leaving the house, William noticed the dark birds perched in a row on the roof. He had grown used to the elation he felt once he left the house, the air that had become thick and difficult to breathe due to the pressure that builds around an aging issue that married couples find impossible to reconcile.

The night before had been particularly trying. William listened but had nothing to say. Mary had come close to telling William that with or without him, she and John George were going to Utah. Instead she had slammed their large wooden serving bowl down on the table hard enough for the green beans in it to rise up a full inch, hanging there, suspended as if time stopped, before falling back into their original position. This level of emotion was new to William. He had looked over to John George, expecting an eye twinkle of support or a wry smile, but for the first time he could remember, his son looked away.

William crossed the road, but before meeting the trail that would take him down along the river, he spotted John Moore, a friend from the pub who was selling the *Evening Star.*

"Why all the birds?" John Moore asked, referring to the starlings that had landed, blackening the branches of a small nearby tree.

"Not sure," William said, wondering if some of them were those he'd seen earlier on his roof.

"Your friend Darwin has made it into the papers, again," John Moore said.

In friendly arguments with Moore about God and life, William sided with the famous naturalist and writer, who'd put Shrewsbury on the map. William had followed Darwin and the controversy surrounding the publication of *On the Origin of Species*, which according to critics—many of whom, like Moore, never actually having read it—suggested that modern humans have monkeys for ancestors.

"What this time?" William asked, in no mood for an argument.

"Smart blokes in Oxford debated the book," John said, beginning to read out loud.

> The soundness or unsoundness of the Darwinian
> Theory gave rise to a long and very animated discussion.
> The Bishop of Oxford, in a speech of great power and
> eloquence, which produced a marked effect upon the
> audience, denounced the theory as unphilosophical, as one
> based upon mere fancy instead of facts, and one which, in
> its effect, was degrading to the dignity of human nature.

"There you have it," John Moore said.
"Is that all?" William asked. John read on.

> Professor Huxley, in reply, alluded to his lordship as an
> "unscientific authority," and then proceeded to defend

> the Darwinian theory in an argumentative speech,
> which was loudly applauded. . . . So far as we could judge,
> the new Darwinian theory, whatever may be its real
> merits in a scientific point of view, has no small number
> of supporters.

"Nothing new here," William said. Among his acquaintances William was in the minority in questioning life and time and modern humans in proper context. He felt a simple kinship with Darwin, knowing a bit about the religious foundation his family had created for him, and then how strong the force of his own experience must have been in order to overcome it. Although he had heard only a fraction of the criticism, prejudice, and even hatred directed at Darwin for his book, William felt for the man. Like Darwin, William marveled at the workings of nature. Unlike Darwin, William was born into, and lived in, circumstances that allowed little time for naturalizing. Like Darwin, he had learned enough to be able to see all religious stories through the same lens—as explanations for natural and mythological phenomena—knowing that the real truth of life existed intact and beautiful at a deep organic level.

William walked down the trail, getting lighter with each step he took along the Severn River. The cowslips were suddenly blooming.

Later that day, John Moore told men at the pub that as William walked away he was followed by a massive flock of black birds forming a long dark ribbon waving in the breeze.

The sea air cooled and William pulled the blanket he'd brought from below tighter around him. "Prayers must be coded," he thought, and chuckled at the notion. Every Sunday early in their marriage he and Mary had prayed together as members of the St. Chad's congregation. He wasn't sure if Mary had continued her prayers or not. He wondered, standing looking down through the green water, how God, who is assumed to be looking down from Heaven, differentiated between the prayers uttered by members of different religions. There must be code words, William thought. Otherwise, why would Mary's recent Mormon prayers trump those she once released into heaven from her seat in St. Chad's Cathedral? Had God heard the right word, the signal for him to inject Mary, to inspire her with the feeling that becoming a Mormon and moving to America was her proper destiny? He chuckled again, recalling a statement Darwin had made to him years before, that humans aren't smart enough to fully comprehend a subject as complicated as God.

William remembered his destiny, the one he sensed that last time he visited Mitchell's Fold.

William's world had changed dramatically since he'd last been to Mitchell's Fold, an ancient circle of stones, a half-day's walk from his home. He'd first visited the stones and heard their story five years before. According to the story, 4,000 years ago this area was suffering from a serious drought, and the local farmers were having a difficult time feeding the people. In this particular village, however, the people had a magic cow that produced what seemed to be an endless supply of milk. They were doing just fine until a witch using her own blend of black magic and a sieve drained the magic cow dry. The villagers caught the offending witch and turned her to stone and then placed her upright in this field. They stood up other stones around her in a circle, creating an eternal prison.

William needed to see the views, the upright stones. He needed to feel the true depth of time once more before leaving for America. He needed Mitchell's Fold not for that story, but to be reminded of the inevitable truth he'd come to understand during his previous visit—the sense thick enough to hold in his hands that the construction of the stone circle was part of his own personal history. His ancestors had tipped those stones into place.

He made the long walk hardly noticing the steps he was taking or rodents moving in the roadside bushes or birds overhead or the clicking sound of mating insects, his head so full of details left to take care of in the month he had remaining. As if he had two minds, one focused on his responsibilities, the other on finding his way, neither aware of the other. Both minds merged as he turned the last bend in the road and saw the stone circle a short distance in front of him.

The cool breeze blowing up from Wales dried his sweat, a product of his long brisk walk. A big cloud that he thought looked more like water floated below him. He moved to the center and paused next to the frozen witch for a moment, looking around. Fifteen stones still stood, half of the original prison, he estimated, the tallest slightly taller than he was—just short of two meters. He'd heard that King Arthur pulled Excalibur out of one of those stones.

Those stones in front of him were closer than those to the side, and he realized he was in the middle of an ellipse, not a circle. He walked around checking for a crack or a hole where a large sword might once have been. Finding none, William sat down, his back resting against the center stone, the solidified witch. The damp ground was cold, but looking out at Wales, he felt happy. He'd escaped, walked beyond the pressure pushing him toward America, if only for a day. The air he breathed in found its way deep into remote parts of his lungs. Wind blowing between stones and the view and four ravens playing with each other in the wind combined to make Mitchell's Fold a very wild place.

William dozed until the cold migrated up into his bones. He got up, brushed off his backside, and turned in a full circle. Then he walked, trancelike, stone to stone to stone, placing his right hand on each one before moving onto the next. He didn't care about what truth might be attached to the milk story, the magic witch, or even King

Arthur. As he touched each stone those stories dissolved, leaving the simple mass and weight mixed with the intangible force of deep and old human connections. He wondered how imagination might be connected to memory, and if a place had a memory. Did those gray stones, upright in the wind, radiate memory of impressions, even the voices they'd absorbed over the centuries, just as they radiated back some of the sun's heat they'd soaked in during the day?

He put both hands on one stone and then pushed against it with all his strength, and it did not move. How many did it take to pick it up and tip it into the hole, he wondered. Why they did this no longer mattered. Is more of the stone above the surface, or below it? He thought about his ancestors again and the very long road that time took to get to him.

Walking back by half-moon light, William realized that he was ready to leave his ancestors, to leave England, to cut himself off from his roots.

Suddenly faint yellow light spattered the dark green sea beneath William, shooting a reflection into his eyes with enough power to overcome his memories and thoughts, dropping him back in the present. Having been missing for days, the sun managed to force its glow through the thick wall of fog. A faint and feeble light beam formed, like liquid, like paint as it thickens, turning to gold only the small wave tips that rose up to meet it.

The light brightened and in the distance, its source appeared—the faint orb of the low sun—the scene first a watercolor becoming an oil painting and in a moment the sun a piece of vivid fruit, close enough to pick from the sky. The weakening fog became the perfect silent contrast. Then light pooled in the sea troughs, and its path, once a small beam, grew and thickened into a golden roadway connecting William directly to the sun.

The fog kept lifting and when William thought that the air should be feeling warmer in the new sun, thick coldness engulfed him. In the foggy distance massive specters appeared as eerie shadows, changing the weather as they drew near. "Icebergs," someone shouted from the stern. They moved closer, almost paradelike, and what had appeared black and white in the distance became many shades of blue, some deep enough to indicate the center of something. Someone would later say that they counted fourteen.

William had never seen an iceberg but knew they were pieces, sometimes gigantic, that had broken away from massive glaciers before floating off on strong ocean currents. He remembered the day Darwin explained the "Bellstone" to him, the familiar erratic stone in downtown Shrewsbury. Erratic, William remembers, unlike any other stones in the area, it had come to rest there when the slow-moving glacier that had carried it across the landscape millennia ago had melted. Darwin had been thinking about glaciers and glacial erratics and how icebergs had been seen recently embedded with a rock to be deposited on some distant shore, far, far from where it originated.

William scanned the iceberg, looking for embedded rocks he would love to tell Darwin about. Finding none he noticed the dark birds roosting on the iceberg's horizontal ledges and that the part of it above the surface of the sea was as big or bigger than the *Cynosure* and, if he squinted, looked like it. Slowly, as one drifted closer to the ship, that ghostlike part of the iceberg beneath the surface came into view. He could find beneath him some of its edges but could not comprehend its depth or in any way its mass. It drifted past the ship as if toward a predetermined destination. First William became the rock embedded in the iceberg being carried away to a distant and foreign land. Then he became the iceberg itself. He'd broken away from his homeland and drifted toward America. All his ancestors were with him, beneath the surface, keeping him afloat.

FIVE

Cottonwood Wash,
San Rafael Desert, Utah

Springtime temperatures had already hit sixty twice, but driving east that day through the San Rafael Swell on I-70, I knew winter had returned to the desert. The late-morning sun thawed the air that shimmered in front of me before striking some distant sandstone boulders, wet from snowmelt, converting them into 50,000-carat diamonds.

I was in a great mood.

Driving that part of I-70 is always spectacular, but that day, cutting through massive cliffs and crossing long plateaus with the light and dancing shadows and dusting of snow, the canyon walls expanded into new dimensions. I was in a good mood because of the beauty and the bright sun, and because I was driving away from Castledale and not toward it. I like Castledale, that sleepy seat of a sleepy county on a highway time left behind, but the meetings I'd been attending there to observe and answer questions from their Public Lands Council were always stressful.

Emery County has a Public Lands Council because like most counties in southern Utah, it is mostly public land—federal land, owned by *all* Americans. The stress results from the disconnect between local and federal control that is bigger than this landscape. For me working with SUWA, this translated very simply: we represent the national interest and believe there to be 1.5 million acres of potential Wilderness in Emery County, while most Emery County residents don't believe in federally designated Wilderness but might be able to live with 400,000 acres, no more, and hopefully a whole lot less. Emery County was in the midst of creating a proposal for a Public Lands Plan that included *some* Wilderness but many more motorized routes and mines and historic sites. To me, representing the rest of America has always involved looking for a balance between the desires of rural counties and the protection of the wilderness qualities that surround them. Often this meant determining what exactly rural people actually need based on current political and economic realities.

To many, the San Rafael Swell is Utah's wild heart, though on the map it's closer to its navel. For most of Utah's population living along the Wasatch Front, Emery County and the San Rafael region is the most accessible big wilderness in Utah. Although I didn't hear anything new at the meeting that morning, I did have two concrete revelations. First, county officials were more willing to kill the process than to commit political suicide by negotiating with SUWA. Second, I will never again argue about what constitutes wilderness. My heart can no longer bear hearing, "Why do you people insist that a place can't be wild if it has dirt roads and motorized vehicles?"

Emery County has tried to pass a number of different land use bills (national monuments, National Conservation Areas, etc.), which gave such little protection to the values held dear by SUWA and our constituents that we mounted serious, successful efforts to squelch them.

This section of I-70 is steep for an interstate as evidenced by emergency escape lanes for trucks that have lost their brakes. I've learned that if I enter the top curve at the proper speed, I can let Ford go. We drop down the south straightaway, letting gravity have its way with us, before flying through the big curve to the east as the freeway exits the massive gap that was blasted through the cliff during construction. I don't touch any pedals. I love the feeling of being spit out of the cliff onto the flats that maps call the San Rafael Desert. It's like being born every time.

Normally I continue east, straight past Green River and onto Highway 191 to Moab. But that day I took the Hanksville exit and drove south. To the west, the lower San Rafael Swell rose up off the desert floor, its multi-colored sandstone layers tilting up into an immense wave that freezes just before breaking. To the east, the San Rafael Desert seemed calm by comparison: short-cliffed mesas and then long, rising vistas broken by the occasional wash and butte. I drove across the San Rafael River knowing that somewhere to the east, the Greater Canyonlands region began and the rest of the world ended.

My destination that day was the area northeast of Hanksville, the rolling desert covered in blackbrush and sage and dissected by a dozen different routes. I needed to know where they go, and why.

I pulled over and checked the map and estimated my turnoff to be fifteen miles away. The dark vegetation seemed to have been dropped from the sky, landing on a perfectly white carpet, the morning's snow melted from any surface not perfectly horizontal.

Lately I'd focused my fieldwork on Greater Canyonlands. Our SUWA mapmakers had drawn a geographically and biologically significant border defining a large area with the official Canyonlands National Park at the center. Geographical boundaries curve and jut. Political boundaries are straight. Straight lines don't exist in Canyonlands or in nature in general, with the exception of the webs of particular spiders or by chance when ice or rocks break.

By 1964, when the U.S. Congress officially created Canyonlands National Park, Secretary of the Interior Stewart Udall had watched political forces cut and gut and chip away at the vision he had for the area since first seeing it in 1961. The same ideology was working then that we fight now: some see protecting any landscape as a threat to their ability to profit from its destruction. Back then Utah's governor, George Dewey Clyde, fought the new national park, its sandstone cliffs and towers. "We're a mining state," he said. "Someday we might need all this as building stone." Now Governor Gary Herbert says we need it for the oil, natural gas, and tar sands and that "Utah is open for business."

Herbert fits right into Utah's conservative political scene. The reddest state in America, Utah's electoral votes are never in question, and nowadays our Democrats need to act like Republicans to stay in office. It's getting worse, not better. Somehow it's easier now, not just in Utah but in the country. We don't need to seriously consider the issues anymore because those leading our parties, both Republican and Democratic, tell us exactly how to think.

I pushed "seek" on my radio and let it spin through the stations, which it did until we were free of the cliffs, when Ford's antenna caught Rush Limbaugh on my radio. I'll listen to Rush once in a while, when nothing else is available. I swear that Fox and Rush and Hannity and the rest of them are available on the radio anytime in any-place in Utah, regardless of its remoteness. It must be a law. Hearing Rush talking to one of his "dittoheads" always makes me think that we may be sub-speciating.

We are members of the species *Homo sapiens* (human who knows) and the subspecies *Homo sapiens sapiens* (human who knows that he knows).

That being true, what would we call the two new subspecies? How about *Homo sapiens selfishi* and *Homo sapiens integradis*—human who is selfish and human who is integrated? Or better yet, *Homo sapiens convergi* / *Homo sapiens divergensis*—convergent and divergent humans?

Much better.

I'd read once that most children are divergent thinkers in that they're more creative and less constrained and see many different possibilities. Adults are more likely to focus on one thing and look only for ideas that support that focus. They converge on one specific idea.

I'd driven Highway 24 fifty times: getting from Moab to Escalante, where I had projects for a few years; or back from river trips that ended at Hite, on Lake Powell; or to hike in the Maze District of Canyonlands National Park. I'd never paid much attention to that part of the road, as I was always on my way to somewhere else. That day was different. I was moving slow, looking for my turnoff. That morning's meeting featured Guy, a towering member of the Public Lands Council who makes his living as a highway patrolman. He represents so-called recreational interests—the motorized crowd, that is. He nearly lost it during a discussion of whether the landscape bisected by Highway 24 had Wilderness qualities. "That's the ugliest stretch of highway on earth," he ranted, his face turning red.

Who gets to say? Beauty has many different dimensions. I wondered if how we see beauty might also have something to do with sub-speciation. It might have just been coincidental that I started thinking about modern humans splitting into subspecies after spending the morning with Guy.

I'd been on a number of field trips with Guy. He definitely feels ownership of these places. He acts entitled. We're diametrically opposed when talk turns to motorized routes. He loves to ride his four-wheeler and, for him, there can never be too many routes. To me, in many places, one route is too many. Once upon a time, long ago and far away, opposing sides might meet, negotiate, compromise by agreeing to close some routes while keeping others open. Now, the opposing sides—on issues involving not just routes or wilderness but nearly everything—are so far apart that any middle ground is unacceptable to everyone.

During field trips we would split up and ride with those with whom we disagree. On one hand, getting to know one another helps us realize that while we disagree about wilderness, we hold much in common—we share more than we don't. On the other hand, the empathy resulting from a deeper understanding often feeds ambivalence. Learning about who they are, what they have, and how they see the world makes it difficult to blame them for hating what I love.

Although none of my colleagues seems to suffer riding with Guy, I never wanted to. He really pisses me off. Like no other rural person, Guy digs under my skin. I can't explain it. I've read enough pop psychology to know that when something about a person drives me crazy, there's a good chance that it's part of my own shadow.

Guy is always quick to say a particular route to a particular viewpoint is legitimate because how else would his brother's mother-in-law be able to get there without a vehicle? Or insist that motors be allowed on the Colorado River because after a long day at work, he and his buddies love to "float down a few miles then motor back home." He's a very angry man. I'd read recently that anger is based on fear. I wondered what he's afraid of. What am I afraid of?

This is what I was thinking headed south, looking for the dirt road leading east into the San Rafael Desert and what the Utah Wilderness Coalition calls the San Rafael River Unit of America's Redrock Wilderness Proposal.

Convergi believes that we're the chosen generation of the chosen species in the chosen country, and that all previous people have existed only for our benefit.

Divergensis lives as part of an infinite system moving toward an unknown future.

Divergensis and *convergi* now speak different languages and have little use for one another. While interbreeding may still be biologically possible, it is unlikely to happen, the two subspecies having lost any attraction to each other.

The softness of the San Rafael Desert—its subtle colors, red, yellow, pink in places, its pure wildness but lack of iconic features—make it a good test for convergence and divergence.

With the signing into law of the Wilderness Act in 1964, 11 million acres in fifty-four different areas were officially designated Wilderness. With some exceptions, places designated during this first phase were big, hundreds of thousands of forested areas and massive peaks, much of it rock and ice. The Bob Marshall Wilderness in Montana, Bridger Wilderness in Wyoming (including key parts of the spectacular Wind River Range), Glacier Peak in Washington's Cascades, and the John Muir Wilderness in the High Sierra of California are good examples. I imagine that some controversy surrounded these designations, but let's face it, there weren't a lot of ideas about how to better use these spectacular places. Those first designated areas fit the key elements outlined in the definition of wilderness within the Wilderness Act: They're big, over 5,000 acres; they're "untrammeled" by man—"trammeled" meaning to catch or hold in or as if in a net, enmesh, or to prevent or impede the free play of; and there we are visitors who do not remain.

During the second phase, a different standard was used to designate wilderness. These places didn't have high peaks with huge, spectacular views but were still wild—with "ecological, geological, or other features of scientific, educational, scenic, or historic value"—as outlined in the act.

The recent Omnibus Public Lands Management Act is a good example.

This law, signed by President Barack Obama in 2009, designated nearly two million acres of Wilderness, much of it in conjunction with national parks, a lot of it in Idaho, some of it in Washington County in the southwest corner of Utah. This did not come easily. After five years of meetings, field trips, flat tires, closed-door negotiations, backroom deals, destroyed partnerships, exploded trusts, and in the end, serious congressional lobbying, Wilderness supporters had what they needed to get 130,000 acres of stark, rugged, diverse, prickly—gorgeous!—desert in southwestern Utah included in this act. The process was like making sausage, but to SUWA the result was palatable.

New designations come hard because the proposed areas don't look like Glacier Peak or Bob Marshall or Wind Rivers—pictures of which have inadvertently and erroneously replaced the definition of Wilderness in the minds of those who oppose further designation of Wilderness. The San Rafael Desert definitely doesn't look like Glacier Peak.

We seem to be entering phase three of Wilderness designations, involving factors often ignored in the definition of wilderness: "land retaining primeval character and influence" that has "substantially unnoticeable" evidence of human impact, and offers "opportunities for solitude." I read this to mean places remote enough or rugged enough to have values we appreciate in proportion to how crowded and noisy, weird, complicated, and wired the rest of our world has become. Besides its unique natural beauty and biodiversity the San Rafael Desert offers rare solitude, threatened by hundreds of miles of roads that exist for the sole purpose of giving motorized recreationists fun, new, and exciting places to ride.

Although there's not much, *convergi* and *divergensis* agree about some Wilderness in southern Utah. But not the San Rafael Desert.

Homo sapiens convergi are found on both sides of this issue. On the right, some see only one aspect of wilderness: big, scenic, untouched areas for which no modern economic use can be found. On the left, after years and thousands of hours and miles and photographs, there are those hardcore Wilderness advocates who have converged on the nearly 10 million acres of land administered by the Bureau of Land Management found to have Wilderness-worthy qualities and are vocally critical of SUWA or any organization that might think about settling for anything less.

Did Howard Zahniser and Olaus Murie, the chief architects of the Wilderness Act, consciously create this three-pronged definition for Wilderness in order to give us what we needed at different times in the future, the way a backpacker might leave a food cache on a long expedition? These phases, for me, define three dimensions of wildness as it applies to life now. The awe we experience in the presence of massive, iconic wilderness taps into the wild yet hidden parts of us. Ecologically and geologically diverse wilderness is made up of an infinite series of intact and complex interconnected systems, which, in my view, is one important definition of wildness. And now, the idea of solitude in wilderness areas becomes the focus at a time when we're all facing planetary problems, when we're on the verge of letting the noise of our own technologies drown out the sound of life itself, including possibly undreamed solutions. Solitude, I believe is the connective tissue between the outer wilderness and our inner wildness, where clues to our long-term survival have always been found.

I slowed down, knowing my turnoff was close, which signaled Rio, who'd been asleep in the passenger seat. Some low-level discomfort had seeped in and had been growing for the past few miles. *Convergi. Divergensis.* A voice in my head asked, "Who do you think you are?" Surely William Williams was the source. I took his question two ways: Who the hell do you think you are to be making such a distinction? But also, Who do you think you are: *convergi* or *divergensis*?

Of course, I'd assumed I was *divergensis*, and Guy the poster child for *convergi*. We split biologically with *Homo sapiens neanderthalensis* 300,000 years ago, becoming *Homo sapiens sapiens.* It took our genus, *Homo*, over 3 million years to get to that point after splitting away from the line that would eventually lead to the great apes, including chimpanzees, our closest living relatives. This type of change comes slowly. As "humans who know we know," we've made some great progress without waiting for help from biology. We've also made major messes, which, because biology is so slow, may require conscious evolution to clean up. A split now may be perfect timing. I wondered whether or not we choose which subspecies we become, based on our actions and beliefs. If we choose, we ought to be able to move from one subspecies to the other.

Our turnoff appeared and we stopped at the closed gate, which was there to keep cows off of the highway. Before getting out to open it, I had to sit there and deal with the discomfort I felt in my gut—waist level, midway between my belt buckle and spine—and to shut William Williams up.

Again, I'm not 100 percent sure that it's actually William Williams and not my conscience, but since meeting him, my conscience has become more specific, directed. Before, its main purpose was to alert me when the line between right and wrong blurred. Now, it—he, William Williams from that other dimension where the dead are doing their best to keep the story going—provides insights, epiphanies, "aha" moments, answers, new questions. There's no other reason I can think of that explains key decisions I've made, the timeliness of particular thoughts, or recollection of important memories. It's been as if I'm being guided along a path toward a goal or destination. For years now, my imagination has been focused, not at all random. William Williams, it seems, died with important unfinished business that he's guiding me to complete.

Sitting there, the bright sun causing me pain, being arrogant about my openness was actually closing me down. Guy and I had more in common than I'd thought. That we had anything in common was more than I'd wanted to admit. "Conscious evolution"—how can this happen? First make the decision to sub-speciate, and then choose *divergensis* over *convergi*.

I shut the engine off and heard a voice echoing in the back of my head. "You're making this up as you go along."

I got out of Ford, shut the door behind me so Rio couldn't escape, and took one full step forward. Thick silence flooded in around my feet. I turned to see if the San Rafael Reef was actually a massive wave from an ancient sea breaking across the valley where I stood. The flood rose around me and I felt myself beginning to float before it retreated as waves do, stripping me of my old dead skin, killed by the morning's meeting, the politics and animosity, killed by Guy.

Free from the dead skin and the deep silence, I moved toward the gate, hearing in my head that the gate was a portal between worlds. William Williams was nearby.

I unclipped the chain and the gate swung open on its own. The route stretched straight east to the horizon, two perfectly white lines of snow. I walked out a few feet, worried about mud beneath the pure snow. I wouldn't want to get stuck out there or to create ruts that might last until fall. Having determined that the ground was firm, I hurried back to Ford, eager to discover what William Williams had in store for me.

Ford skimmed along the soft snow cushion. Underneath the tracks were smooth ruts, deep enough to guide my truck, and I thought about rigging the gas pedal to keep it going while I climbed up on top to sit and watch the desert go by. That would be stupid, I thought, remembering a story: two friends would put their four-wheel-drive Dodge Power Wagon in low-range gear and climb on top with their beer and ride across the desert at one mile per hour. They barely escaped serious injury once when they were thrown off after their truck broke through a barbed-wire fence and crashed into a ditch.

The road climbed gradually before dropping into a wide dry wash. The map showed the main route heading north and a short spur to the south. Without thinking, I turned south into the wash and followed old tracks through loose sand, the snow all but gone. I hit the gas hoping not to bog down—I've spent too many hours stuck, digging out of deep sand. We made it easily up through a cut in the bank and onto solid ground. The road angled toward a high cliff and then along the base, ending when it turned back on itself in a large cove. A carefully maintained fire ring, pieces of unburned firewood, and a pile of old rusted cans suggested a popular camping spot. I let Rio out and he immediately went to work getting to know the decades of campers and all the dogs who had stayed there. After two hours in meetings and another in the truck, we needed to walk. I climbed between the loose barbed-wire strands of a fence built for no reason that I could tell. I stiffened in the cold breeze and huge clouds moved on, dragging the last of that morning's storm east.

We found a footpath between wash and cliff, which we followed until it disappeared onto a slickrock ledge. There, the cliff blocked the wind and the rocks radiated the warmth from recently absorbed sun, all of it together creating a soft and private world. I looked around for the right perch knowing I wanted to stay a while. I knew we were not the first to want to spend a while there.

Finding the south-facing cliff face covered with petroglyphs did not surprise me. Around me I found thin flecks that a thousand years before had been chipped away from large blanks exposing the atlatl points, scrapers, and knives the maker had mysteriously seen within. I had no trouble imagining a small band of archaic hunter-gatherers living there.

I found a perfect place to sit—smooth bedrock for my butt with a boulder for the small of my back, angled perfectly for a view of the landscape expanding in front of me and of the clouds above.

Time loses its form in unchanged places. It's no longer linear. It no longer progresses. It may be circular, but sitting there that day, I thought about time spiraling. As time moves, it revisits wild places. A thousand years passed between the time the people who made the rock art were camped there and my visit. I sat against the same rock looking at the same view, glancing west, just as he did, toward the horizon where change comes from, trying to read tomorrow's weather in the clouds. We may have pondered the same question, that man forming a spear point with a tool made from a deer antler and I: what do we need to get through the coming dark period? The camp hadn't changed, but the universe had added a dimension and moved it closer to the future.

I've long envied Navajo and Hopi people I know for their ceremonies and rituals and the sacred dimension they see in all life. Mainly I envy their ancestral relationship to places I've come to love and want to protect. Connecting with people from another time has always been a key element of my wilderness experience.

For a long time I wondered how much more connected I might feel standing in an ancient Celtic stone circle in western England or eastern Wales, where my ancestors were born. Before leaving for England to learn more about William Williams, I read books on European prehistory and discovered that the Celtic people are considered native European. To traditional Celtic people, places have a soul, a spirit or personality. They have a phrase for this place-soul: *anima loci.* Celtic beliefs and traditions are expressed spiritually through the landscape, which is filled with places where spirits are present. They believe that each time we experience a sacred, spirit-filled place, we're encouraged to make an imaginative act that personifies that particular place to us. That personality is its *anima loci. Anima loci,* a powerful force, makes places sacred.

Discovering that I too have a native history comforted me. That all native people, no matter where they are or were, or who they are or were, or when, share many common traits. Key among them is a deep relationship to the land—something we all shared once. Native is native.

I loved England, the green hills and immense fields outlined by stone walls. What the massive quoits and dolmens, stone circles, and dark tombs did to my imagination I might never fully know. The *anima loci*? I felt it and heard it in England, but no louder there than sitting with that rock art in that ancient camp. No more than any wild place on the Colorado Plateau.

In England I had one simple epiphany: I'd gone thousands of miles to visit the place where my ancestors were born only to realize that just because my genealogy showed my earliest ancestors showing up there in the late 1700s, they didn't just fall out of the sky. *My ancestors had ancestors*—who had ancestors who had ancestors—going back to those first cells coming alive in that steamy swamp. For the first time I saw my family tree as a small branch connected to the entire massive tree of life.

We've drawn the boundary between our personal and collective history, as if we're somehow different from our ancestors, special, "exceptional." We're all related if we're willing to look back far enough.

In my mind I heard the deep grinding of seeds between stones—the mano and metate—the hand-stone that after many years of use fits the flat plate-stone perfectly. And the three laughing children chasing each other with willow whips, the singing, and the cracking and popping of burning piñon in the fire. What happens to sound over the centuries? Where does it go? With the art-covered wall, the camp, and the scattered lithics left from tool-making, that my imagination accurately filled in those sounds makes complete sense. Carving figures through the dark patina on that sandstone wall—what sounds must that have made? Were those lines scraped or chiseled?

Whenever I encounter rock art, I feel time shrink. I feel the distance between the past and the present disappearing. Time thins out. For me, rock art sites are thin places. All wild places may be thin places.

To my Celtic cousins, thin places are those where the distance between the sacred and the secular, heaven and earth, the spiritual and the physical, is small. Wilderness may be as close as many ever get to places where this great blending is still possible: heaven with earth, the spiritual with the physical, the past with the present. Civilization thickens the divider, increases the distance.

People spend their lives trying to understand and document the thousands of rock art sites scattered all over the Colorado Plateau. They have many diverse theories, but with rock art, mystery grows faster than knowledge. I've spent hundreds of hours watching rock art. Where once I tried understanding what it meant, now I look at it and wonder in the same way I look at a painting by Picasso or Miró and see what is vaguely familiar in a different, exciting, unknown context. I love knowing that regardless of what it says to me, to the artist who produced it the art makes absolute sense and is filled with pure meaning.

Was rock art created for its function, or is it simply the artist's creative expression? Some believe that the shaman—the religious leader—created the rock art as communication with the spirit world, which would mean that it is filled with information and guidance. I have friends who believe that a rock art panel is a map of the surrounding landscape.

The quiet sounded as if the earth was relaxing—exhaling. With the sun out heating the rock and plants and soil, everything once clenched with cold began to loosen. My seat was perfect, and knowing that any movement would disrupt the solitude, I sat still. I read that the first people to meditate were primitive hunters waiting for game. This suggests that when not meditating we must be sending signals—waves or some other form of energy—rippling out into the solitude, like a stone thrown into a quiet pond. Those waves not only repel animals but must also mask any signs that the natural system constantly whirs on unencumbered, reacting to anything that might interrupt the flow of life. No wonder with all the cement and steel, all the electronic signals we're constantly swimming in, we've forgotten the natural system even exists, let alone still completely controls our modern lives.

I hated to get up, but Rio had disappeared and I needed to see what he was up to. I found him in a perfect sun puddle chewing a deer leg—complete with hoof. We needed to get going to make the highway by dark. I walked off knowing exactly when Rio would pass me, the deer leg dangling from his mouth, and I was right. He sprinted ahead to feast more on the leg in peace. We leapfrogged like that all the way back to Ford.

He didn't bring the leg into the truck.

Imagine how it must have been to live an entire life—all of it—in the wild. All of it hunting deer or bighorn sheep, or gathering edible plants. I love being out more than most people but can't imagine not having a warm house and cupboard full of food to go back to.

Nowadays, our needs for food and shelter and safety are met. We've got extra space in our lives, which modern civilization is there to fill with television, movies, professional sports. Civilization is good at helping us decide who we want to be but not at helping us discover who we innately are. This system seems designed to separate us from the sacred and convince us that the past is irrelevant. Thin places are bad for business.

What went through the minds of our ancient ancestors? I imagine a deep knowledge having nothing to do with memory and requiring no thought. A knowledge that opened when signaled—by changes in the weather or the position of the sun rising and falling at different times of the year, by irregular movements in the corners of their eyes or the scent of close, large mammals in the shifting breeze. Books published recently advocate the use of ancient teachings in modern life. They share the idea that what we think is only a small part of the information available to us. The popularity of these books suggests that many among us are beginning to see that too much thinking has played a role in getting us into trouble, and that more thinking is unlikely to get us out.

Although I'm working on it, back home I struggle to duplicate the calm that comes over me in wild and quiet places like the San Rafael Desert. I long for the twists and turns my imagination takes when set free for a few days in the wild desert.

Imagine the effect constant quiet and expansive views had on the imaginations and creativity of people living their entire lives immersed in wildness.

The people who lived in what is now southern Utah were some of the last of our species to live as nomadic hunters and gatherers, a way of life that worked very successfully for 200,000 years. Their success may have been based on imagination and creativity grounded in instinct and impression rather than a vault of personal memory. Our survival may require relearning what modern life has forced us to forget.

"Rio, where the hell are you?" I yelled back along the path. I turned to open Ford's door and almost crashed into my dog coming from the opposite direction. He jumped in, without a clue as to what was next but ready for anything.

We drove back the way we came—along the cliff, into and out of the sandy wash and back up the hill to the last junction. In the months since starting this project to ground-truth wilderness maps, I'd been taking pride in finding large blank spaces on the maps and then getting to know them on the ground. I was building equity. To look out on nothing but open, wild space as far as I could see was to imagine what those who spent their entire lives in this land knew about it that I didn't. Primitive hunters in Alaska draw maps of their homeland as accurately as modern cartographers using aerial photographs.

Theories based on nomadic people still living hunting-gathering lives in the world's most remote places suggest that our primitive ancestors didn't move randomly throughout the land but had regular routes, stopping in familiar places for the length of time it took to deplete the resources they required. I don't believe in the Noble Savage idea which holds that our primitive ancestors lived more thoughtfully with regard to the earth and its resources. Restraint must be a recent concept, surely not innate. We took full advantage of any resource we were able to find at any time. For this to go on for as long as it did, a nearly perfect balance must have existed between the resources available, the numbers of people requiring them, and the technology to extract them. That balance is gone. Our population continues to grow, and the technologies we're using to feed and fuel the world are killing us. I watched the San Rafael Reef catch fire from the setting sun.

SIX

Big Draw,
Canyonlands National Park, Utah

For the next few weeks I focused my fieldwork on the part of Greater Canyonlands north of the park, east of the Colorado River. Our maps of the area are completely depressing. Red lines delineate routes the Bureau of Land Management has designated as open for travel but that are in conflict with potential Wilderness. The map looks like the bloodshot eye of a drunken man.

Every BLM field office functions according to its Resource Management Plan, a part of which is the Travel Plan, which consists of maps of all the routes and what they can and cannot be used for. Recently Moab has gained fame for its mountain biking, but for far longer it has been the mecca for motorized recreation. In their four-wheel drives, motorcycles, and now all-terrain vehicles (ATVs)—those annoying modified golf carts that can go anywhere—and rock crawlers (motorized buggies custom-built to crawl around on rocks), the motorheads defile the delicate desert, turning it into their playground.

Although most visitors to the Moab area come for quiet travel—hiking, sightseeing, etc.—the motorheads are the most vocal, and noisy, and wield the most political power.

A subset of people in love with their motors have much in common with the faction of those in love with their guns. Masculinity seems directly related to both motor and gun size. Members of both are single-issue people, equating the American freedom they were promised by being born here with their ability to own and use either. Any effort to limit such a person's right to use his gun or his jeep is seen as an infringement on his inalienable rights, and too much government control could seed a revolution. It's that serious. Just as serious gun enthusiasts who believe that outlawing even one type of assault weapon is the first step toward outlawing all guns, motorheads are convinced that closing even one route means that all routes are soon to suffer the same fate.

Recently, when the BLM began working on its current travel plan, Moab's political elite presented them with a map of all the routes to be officially designated as open to motorized travel.

That map had 23,000 route segments.

The BLM controls massive amounts of land on which they must balance a nearly impossible list of "multiple uses," including mining, oil and gas extraction, ranching, all types of recreation, wilderness, endangered species, water, and others. The people working in BLM field offices are constantly barraged by community members focused on one specific use. Regardless of what is best for the land, the BLM staffers are only human and often make decisions based on their own personal biases, pressure they receive from their neighbors and friends, or members of their Mormon congregation. This does not bode well for places like Moab, where many of the multiple uses the locals support often conflict with wilderness values.

The BLM had a problem. In order to properly do their job protecting land belonging to all Americans, they couldn't automatically designate all 23,000 segments. Doing so would incite SUWA, the Grand Canyon Trust, Living Rivers, or any of a dozen other groups to collectively jump down their throats.

After a lot of head scratching the BLM decided that since they had neither the time nor the resources to physically check each of the 23,000 routes, they would use a statistical test. Complex formulas showed that if 451 of those 23,000 routes were legitimate—meaning they were often used, and had a destination, etc.—there was a 95-percent chance that all 23,000 were legitimate.

Having neither the time nor the resources to physically check even 451 routes, the BLM found aerial photographs taken in 1990, which were used for confirmation. The result was a travel plan with most of the 23,000 routes—many of them doing serious damage to the definition of the word *route*—designated as open to motorized travel.

Although tedious, our job at the Southern Utah Wilderness Alliance was simple. We needed to create sufficient doubt by demonstrating that a significant number of those designated routes were, in fact, not legitimate, and would do that by photographing them at ground level instead of from 25,000 feet.

I assembled a system consisting of an attachment for the camera that embeds GPS coordinates into a photo's metadata and software that "flies" that data onto Google Earth, enabling the viewer to see the route from above, simulating an aerial photograph. Then by clicking an icon, the viewer can see what that route actually looks like on the ground.

Contrary to what our opponents would have you believe, we do not want every dirt road in every Wilderness unit closed. Much wilderness in southern Utah is only accessible by long dirt roads. You can drive your Subaru with your aging grandparents to some of the wildest, most remote wilderness in Southern Utah.

By noon I'd taken two dozen photos of four different routes in the Horsethief area just north of the Canyonlands National Park border. I'd walked three or four miles noting anything that interrupted the wildness.

It was a week short of the equinox but still spring in the desert after a long moist winter. Not much had bloomed, but I felt life revving up outside my open window.

As usual Rio was with me. So was William Williams.

We stopped to check my GPS and mark my map where an orange swath through the sand forked west between dense blackbrush. The road beyond was steep and rocky and, based on the virginal winter-formed delicate crust, hadn't been driven on in months or years, even though the BLM map showed it as a "designated" route.

I stepped down from the truck and stood on a large, flat slickrock outcropping—not a lick of wind, and thick silence textured like deep dry snow filled the air. Above me, raven wings slicing up the air was the only sound. Without warning, the term "ground-truth," which had always been a verb meaning what I do with maps as part of my job, became a noun. It meant the truth coming up from the ground.

I credited that insight to William Williams, my long-dead ancestor. Mystical or spiritual rather than rational or scientific, it happened and I could not explain it away by what I'd eaten for breakfast combined with the sweet, new air. In our early days as a species, when we had very little scientific proof to go on, stories and myths contained the rules to live by and described life and the way it works. Now, we have two choices: either we find and create stories to help us explain what remains unknown, or we embrace the real myth, which is that we now know everything.

Meeting William marked a subtle but major shift in my wilderness experience. Before, I was drawn by adventure. I moved fast and far, too fast to hear the ground-truth. The ground-truth changed everything.

I put water and food and Rio's jerky in my pack, locked Ford, hid the key, and walked west, the sun warm on my back. Ford could have easily negotiated the legal road as it continued on from where we'd parked, but we love to walk and wouldn't want our truck tracks to in any way legitimize this route, which if I were successful in my mission, no one would ever drive again.

The dirt under my feet was so soft I might have been floating. A sweet scent rode the mild breeze—a juniper or blackbrush barely waking up. All around me the ground stretched and breathed, getting ready to move. Small birds flitted about, and one solitary black fly with at least a dozen acres to itself took a curious lap around my head. My aging knees and hips quickly remembered how much they love to walk as the soft desert and motion dissolved all kinks and pain. My route barely slanted downward, and the solitude melted and flowed and carried me along. I didn't leave a ripple.

Rio was ahead of me. Besides his, the only tracks had been left by a small rodent, perhaps an antelope ground squirrel. Just as the map said it would, the route ended, turning back on itself. According to his tracks, Rio had gone south, toward the wash I knew drained into a gash in the rim that dropped into Canyonlands National Park.

I followed Rio's tracks as they wove among the sage and the prickly pear, giving them a wide berth, then down through a break in the short vertical wall caused by a flood that had recently flashed through the wash.

The bottom of the wash had been carved by wind and water, and without scale it looked like a miniature view of the greater surrounding terrain that I might get from a plane high above. There, carpet-sized beneath me, lay sensuous domes of blown sand, sharp ridges, and layers of varied thickness, all cut earlier by water, the complete and fantastic story of how the landscape I loved came to be. I found Rio lying at the base of a giant rabbitbrush, its leaves barely hinting green.

I dug a soft place to sit in, and in no time spring's first warm air pulled off my shirt and sandals and sucked my bare feet deep into the cool sand.

Once my mind slowed down and I'd settled into my sand hole, the dream I'd had just before dawn that morning came flying back to me. It was not a dream as much as a familiar voice, a statement pronounced in my head soft and deep, as if echoed from the back of a long cave:

"When the books have gone, open midnight."

I must have gone back to sleep right after because I hadn't thought about that phrase until half the day had passed.

"Which books?" I wondered as the cloud shadow shaped like a bent star moved across the wash in front of me.

During the months leading up to the spring day in that wash, I'd started to feel like I was making progress toward understanding the meaning of wilderness and exactly how it saves us. For decades I'd gathered ideas from a small group of writers and thinkers who had all contributed to my knowledge and formed my intellectual foundation. The day before that dream I'd wondered if that stack of their books on my bedside table had gone beyond a foundation and had become a prop to lean against or, worse yet, a wall to hide behind.

I knew which books. Very well.

I thought of *The Dominion of the Dead*, by Robert Pogue Harrison. I picked it off a shelf in a Paris bookshop not long after meeting William, and on page one found just enough information to keep me from thinking I was nuts, which is the best reason for buying any book. The dead, Harrison suggests, are around us all the time—in a separate reality. They have a relationship with the unborn, and it's their responsibility to encourage the living to "keep the story going." The dead need the living to preserve their authority, to fuel their afterlives. In exchange, they provide help for us beyond their graves.

Harrison described to a tee the role William played in my life—his contributing to my ideas, influencing my thoughts, directing my attention. For me, this meant that in some form William is still alive, that there is life after death.

Either you believe in life after death or you don't, which has nothing to do with whether or not there is life after death. There either is or there isn't, regardless of what we think or believe.

If you don't believe in life after death, so be it.

If you do believe we might live in some form after death, things get interesting.

My sense is that the dead live on in some alternate form, that they're concerned about the future. Harrison says that they want to "keep the story going."

Growing up Mormon, we were taught that life continues after death but only after Christ comes back. Since we've not been cremated and we've been buried in our Temple Clothes, and we were good during our lives, we'll all rise up from our graves, complete and beautiful, and head off to reign over our own planets. I always thought this seemed too perfect—a way to control us by promising a reward in the hereafter.

Discovering that William Williams was part of my life turned any previous ideas I'd had about life after death upside down, and reading *Dominion of the Dead* helped me make some sense of it.

Darwin's *Voyage of the Beagle* had been on my list the longest. What an adventure! When I read it as a college freshman, it inspired me to pursue biology, if only as the means to experiencing and better understanding more of nature's wonders. Today I'm amazed to think that young Charles walked onto that ship believing in the literal interpretation of the Bible—a male, talking, vengeful God and seven days of creation and fire and brimstone and all of it. But five years later, back home in England, he walked off the *Beagle* believing differently. What he saw happening in the wild world—the Galápagos, Tierra del Fuego, etc.—had made the difference. His personal experience in nature trumped any belief he'd developed secondhand.

My uncle J. D. and my aunt Bea gave me *Religions, Values, and Peak Experiences,* by Abraham Maslow, as a gift when I graduated from college in 1974. I wasn't sure why. Years later when I actually read it, I understood what had happened to me: why I hadn't and couldn't and shouldn't embrace the lifestyle my family and culture had planned for me. Maslow had interviewed thousands of people who claimed to have had a "peak experience" and found many common themes. Just as with *Dominion of the Dead,* Maslow's book gave me words and context for my own story, helped me better understand my own life, and let me know that I am not alone

C. A. Meier gave a speech at the 1984 World Wilderness Conference (it's called "Wilderness and the Search for the Soul of Modern Man" and is found in Meier's book, *Soul and Body: Essays on the Theories of C. G. Jung).* These sentences stood out as if highlighted in bright yellow: "The wilderness within would really go 'wild' if we should badly damage the outer wilderness. So let us keep the balance as best we can, in order to maintain sanity." I came of age in the wilderness movement among many people who believed that wild places needed protection, whether or not people ever got to see them. I knew what wandering around in wild places did for me mentally, physically, emotionally, but reading Meier was a major step toward seeing the connection between wilderness and the direct role it plays in our modern lives.

Meier was a student of Carl Jung. Terry's grand-mother, Mimi, introduced me to Jung back in the late 1970s. By immersing herself in Jung, along with Thomas Merton, Maslow, Jiddu Krishnamurti, and Alan Watts, Mimi had inadvertently "read" herself out of the Mormon Church. Whenever Terry and I would travel with her, Mimi insisted that we spend breakfast discussing dreams we might have had the night before. This was my intro-duction to Jung and his theories about archetypes and the collective unconscious.

Mimi gave me her books before she died in 1989.

In one of them, *Memories, Dreams, and Reflections*, Carl Jung said that, while he loved the outer world, explor-ing the inner world was more exciting and gave his life the most meaning.

Jung held that the outer, everyday world is the con-scious world, while the unconscious world of dream and shadow and archetype is the inner world. I'd coupled that idea with the statement Paul Shepard made in his classic *Nature and Madness* about civilization being a veneer, within which is the core human we all evolved to be. This connection became clearer still once I realized that Jung's collective unconscious was not a mystical but a biologi-cal phenomenon, and that its archetypes are biological entities subject to natural selection and inherited just as genes are inherited. To me, Shepard and Jung were saying the same thing, although from the different disciplines of biology and psychology, blurring any line separating the two.

Known as the father of human ecology, Shepard wrote passionately and constantly about the problems caused by forcing our bodies, unchanged since the Pleistocene, to live in a world vastly different from the one for which evolution designed us. Reading Shepard calmed me down when I found a familiar context, and suddenly what I was doing and thinking and feeling started making sense. While I loved exploring the core of the earth—the wild parts not yet covered by civilization's spreading and thickening veneer—it was the core of myself, my own inner workings, stirring, sending me dreams and impressions and ideas that I'd been unable to reconcile before finding Shepard.

Along came Meier, who miraculously connected my "inner" unconscious world to the wilderness. Being a visual person—I was the kid who needed an actual coconut cream pie to learn fractions—I'd diagrammed Shepard's veneer/core concept as a small circle within a larger one, only to realize that it applied to the earth as well as to our personal lives. The outer civilized world of farms, cement, and pavement covered the wild natural world. Wilderness became places on the earth where the veneer was absent, or at least thin enough to move through. Wilderness areas became thin places for me, with minimal distance between the spiritual and the secular, the past and the present, heaven and earth.

In *The Earth Has a Soul: C.G. Jung on Nature, Technology and Modern Life*, Meredith Sabini, a Jungian psychologist from Berkeley, has compiled pieces from Jung's work and written a brilliant essay to go with them. I happened across this book while snooping around a friend's house where I was staying. I didn't realize how important Jung considered his time in the natural, wild world. I inhaled that book. I talked to Dr. Sabini about the connection I imagined between biology and psychology; she said that the core or inner world is biological—"evolutionary material," she calls it. It holds "the entire evolutionary history of our species," she says. She believes that within the collective unconscious can be found all the tools our species has ever needed to save itself.

It made sense to Sabini that our inner world aligns perfectly with the earth's core—the wild places civilization has yet to cover or seal off. And while psychologists, yogis, and poets are getting better at finding access to that unconscious, evolutionary material, the wilderness—the quiet, wild places where natural systems are still intact and obvious—can be a portal between worlds.

Dr. Sabini told me that I was an example of what she and her colleagues had been noticing recently. "That people as naïve as you are beginning to think about these ideas," she said, "suggests that the collective unconscious is rising to the surface in unexpected places. This always happens whenever our species has been in trouble." I took that as a compliment.

The surfacing of the collective unconscious when we're in trouble suggests that if we were more comfortable with the collective unconscious and better at accessing it, we would more likely be engaged in efforts to save our species rather than in those that threaten us.

I'd made enough sense for one day and still had some routes to check. Plus, I couldn't think of any more books and the air had cooled and I needed to move. I found Rio stretched out sound asleep in a hole he'd dug. I tried sneaking up on him but only got within five feet when he jumped up, looking a little embarrassed, as if he'd been shirking his dog duty of standing guard for me.

Reminded that time moves at many different speeds and not always in one direction, we got back to Ford much more quickly than expected. We drank some water, climbed in, and drove off.

When the books have gone, open midnight.

The books weren't really gone, but, in my mind, just listing them meant taking down the stack, the monument I'd made of them. Once again they became something to read rather than worship. I no longer needed them to lean against or stand behind. But "open midnight"—what the hell did that mean?

I doubt that I'd be thinking about ground-truth as a noun had I not been out on that slickrock on that spring day. And I wonder if I'd have recalled that dream about

Ground-truth

books and midnight if, instead of driving out into the desert, I had gone into my office to work. And if the dead are really out there somewhere, eager to help us, perhaps they get through to us more easily in thin places—in the wilderness. Ground-truth—the ground telling us the only real truth there is.

These were not isolated events. That day was unique in place and content, but the simple, profound, and un-mistakable feeling that a ground-truth—a new clue to life, another bread crumb along the path, a small piece of the large truth puzzle—had been revealed was familiar.

When the books have gone, open midnight.

Midnight. Yes, 12:00 exactly, but also halfway be-tween sunset and sunrise. It's the exact point when one day changes to the next. And that vast unconscious world where important secrets are hidden. Midnight is the end-ing of one thing and the beginning of something else.

SEVEN

Platte River,
Somewhere in Middle America

Walking, striding while inhaling breath into the bottom of his lungs, lighting up dark rooms in his body unopened since those last days in England. William recognized that rhythm.

He followed a well-worn path along the river's edge, its elements combining into a memory of walking back home, along the Severn, a smaller river, but similar in color and strength. After two months of travel—most of it aboard a ship crossing the Atlantic—his legs were foreign countries. From a strap over his shoulder hung his dead father's leather satchel, where he kept documents, money he'd borrowed to make the journey, and the two books his friend Charles Darwin had given him.

After leaving Liverpool in May, the packet ship *Cynosure* landed in New York on July 19. The city was in turmoil, with thousands of troops roaming the smoke-filled streets across which young men darted like predators. From a discarded copy of the *New York Times* the group learned of the terrible rioting nearby, protests against the drafting of young men to replace the tens of thousands being killed in that mysterious Civil War.

> As if by preconcerted action an attack was made upon colored men and boys in every part of the city during the day, crowds of from 100 to 500 persons hunting them like bloodhounds. Several inoffensive colored men were dragged off the city cars and badly beaten, while a number were taken from carts and drays which they were driving and terribly maltreated. (*New York Times*, July 14, 1863)

Williams knew little of that war or of slavery, for that matter. Or that a number of states wanted to secede, to break free of America, a country to which he'd now committed the rest of his life. He didn't think about history and couldn't have known that for decades to come the Civil War years would be seen as America's darkest.

William knew he and his family and the souls they'd traveled with from England were part of the Mormon Migration. He couldn't have known that when it ended thirty years later, 85,000 Saints would have made similar journeys from Europe to America. While he might have guessed that he and his family and the Mormon Migration would change history, he couldn't have known that the role they played would be seen as a major factor in America's Manifest Destiny. Or that the phrase "Manifest Destiny" refers to much more than a plan for moving people west to take advantage of the abundant resources to be found there. Although the term was first used in an 1845 article describing the God-given responsibility of white Christians to occupy the North American continent south of Canada, the idea can be traced to the seventeenth century. English settlers were told by their Christian clergy that they'd been charged by God to make an "errand into the wilderness" of America, which He had chosen for a special destiny. They were to continue converting New World natives to Christianity, a process that began with the "discovery" of America by Christopher Columbus. God pronounced America exceptional: the end-times that would usher Christ back to earth would begin in America. Tame the wilderness. Subdue the native people. Spread God's word. Prepare for the end.

The missionaries would have explained to William that this was the reason that Mormons were called Latter-day Saints. He was told that Salt Lake City was the Holy City in the Wilderness from which Saints would spread the gospel, first throughout the entire country and then the world, and that America would be the site of the Millennium.

Potential converts learned from the missionaries that the Mormon Church is the one true church on earth, and Saints who obey all the commandments and are worthy will one day live like God, each on his or her own planet. While the rewards possible after death were significant, the promises of a new life in Utah before death provided the stronger incentives for most. The missionaries promised potential converts five things: Zion, a sanctuary from the desolation that was sure to sweep over the ungodly world in the last days; land, all the land one could reasonably cultivate; gainful employment; association with fellow believers; and equal opportunity with the "best people."

Whether the missionaries promised a loan to make the trip early in their conversations or later as part of their last offer, William borrowed thirty-nine British pounds from the Perpetual Emigration Fund, thirteen each for the three of them.

From New York City they were taken to Albany, where they caught a train to St. Joseph, Missouri, riding with soldiers being moved to more strategic positions from which to fight the ongoing war. The system designed to get converts from England to Utah was tried and tested, thousands having gone before William, Mary, and fifteen-year-old John George. In Florence they purchased the supplies the last leg of their journey would require. There they met the covered wagon that would transport their lives to Utah and the two oxen that would pull it.

John George was happy to have the responsibility of walking on the left side of the ox-team, which seemed to know the way, and Mary was content to walk beside him, talking, William was free to find his own way. Often he followed the animal paths between the main trail and the river. At times he would have to hurry to catch up, realizing that solid silence had replaced the creaking of fifty moving wagons and three hundred voices. He'd lingered too long sitting on a log dreaming or following the sound of a large invisible animal moving through the underbrush.

Although William knew little about most things, he felt strangely at home wandering along the Platte River among the sounds of invisible birds moving in the bulrushes and tall fuzzy-headed grasses rubbing against one another. He watched motionless, long-necked birds waiting for fish to stab with their dartlike beaks. Smaller, stilt-legged birds poked the mud for food. Brilliant blue dragonflies hunted midges just like in England. He heard the click and buzz of three different insects, which although invisible, unknown, and American, grounded him. If he lived to be a hundred, he thought, he would never forget that moment when the sun disappeared and the sky filled with the combined thunder of a billion black birds, each one like a single stitch in a giant's dark cloak rippled by the wind. Perfect V formations of geese flew close enough for William to make out their white chin straps. "My ravens," he said the first time he saw them, ecstatic that they'd followed him from home, although sure that they hadn't.

The river always in sight to his left, he could wander free-minded, something he'd grown fond of doing back home. During those last desperate years leading up to this new life, his life depended on wandering, as he contemplated his future and unknown destiny. He'd missed his body during the long sea voyage, but walking loosened his mind, and the possibility and promise that had lain inside, trapped in the dark, flew out like once-caged birds.

This was serious, he thought, moving slowly. During the long voyage several died and were buried at sea, a sack of coal tied to their feet. Several were born. Yet the hardest part of the journey was in front of them.

As he walked along he told himself the story he was living in: how it began, whether it was one specific detail of the missionary discussions that had changed his mind or that he had simply been worn down by years of debating and arguing with Mary and forced, finally, to choose family over place. He had given in, but had he given up? During those years, he'd become articulate about what he'd known for decades—the importance of home. Long ago he'd grown sick of feeling stuck there in that shabby neighborhood, his mindless work, with little chance for change. Until the Mormons came knocking on his door, any chance for change lay dormant in the depth of his own heart.

During those years between the missionaries showing up at their door and walking onto that ship with his family, William had escaped his home during downtime to avoid further discussion about leaving England. During his long walks along the Severn River his appreciation grew for the subtle natural changes induced by the combination of season and weather. He kept track of what attracted his attention—shadows moving across his path, particular insects or birds, mice that seemed to flirt with him, dappled light he caught in the palm of his hand. Some days, and they were rare, he could not differentiate his walking thoughts from his night dreams.

Perhaps his age was a factor or his weariness from both the bantering and his endless toil, but he was no longer interested in leaving, in exploring places he'd spent his life imagining. He'd come to believe that most of what he'd been looking for was much closer than he'd thought. On the surface this chance in Utah seemed to be all he'd ever hoped for—the promise of a new life in a new place. But this new life required new beliefs conflicting with those rooted in his own experience and filtered through what he was slowly learning about life and how it worked.

He watched the clouds as he walked. For the first time, he didn't need them to look like anything—not a clown's face, a sailboat, or the vicar's hat—only appearing, moving, building, disappearing.

EIGHT

Musée d'Orsay, Paris

In March we went to Paris on vacation. The day before leaving I'd returned from the Grand Staircase–Escalante National Monument, where I'd been documenting routes Garfield County officials claimed they'd maintained because they were necessary to the local economy.

Paris is as far from Escalante, Utah, as it could possibly be, in size, aesthetic, and wildness. I love them both, Escalante and Paris. This was my second trip to Paris with Terry, and I'd been looking forward to food and museums but also to unstructured time to sit in coffee shops reading and writing in my notebook. At some point in my life, museums had become almost unbearable—the pain of standing inside, trying to concentrate on each amazing art piece. After an hour my back and knees start killing me and I get dizzy and feel faint. I suspect I'm overstimulated. As I get older the aesthetic brilliance of what I experience in a museum can be nearly offset by the suffering I'm required to endure. Knowing I was going to Paris, I devised a plan for getting the most from museums—the Louvre, the Musée d'Orsay, L'Orange. I would be more selective about what I looked at. I would plan my museum visit as I would a wilderness trip, with a beginning and an end, with an exciting route between them.

D'Orsay was first. Rather than barging through the entrance and wandering aimlessly, I sat and mapped my route, noting in the catalog the locations of those pieces I wanted to see. For the first hour everything went according to plan. I'd seen some amazing photographs—Muybridge, Steichen, and Stieglitz—on the main floor, Salle 19, and had walked up the stairs to look first at the flowing bodies of Rodin's most beautiful work, *Fugit Amor*. To get to my next stop, the Van Goghs in Salle 71, I needed to be on the other side of the atrium. I heard William's voice either from behind or inside me, and although I'd planned to turn right, my body went left. I kept moving, pulled by an invisible cord, knowing, somehow, that something was about to happen. The next moment I was trapped in a mysterious force field emanating from a huge painting hanging on a distant wall. Every element of that painting glowed in minute detail. From a distance, I saw a group of my friends moving intently across a wild slickrock landscape beneath the cliffs west of Escalante. While the people in the painting could have been my friends, they were not. Not exactly. Looking closer at the shades of red and orange and the distance by dark vertical cliffs—the landscape was less familiar than I first thought. In the painting a taut and bent older man led a number of muscular young men. Some carried a woman and her babies on a large wooden stretcher. Others had the carcasses of animals they'd killed draped over their shoulders. One held a young girl in his arms. Wild dogs followed close behind to snatch falling scraps. The situation appeared tense. A turbulent sky pulled a giant shadow across the landscape. The group seemed to be looking for shelter ahead of the coming storm.

The longer I looked at the painting, the thicker the air in the room became. Time slowed and crowds of sleepwalkers surrounded me. I felt wildness—the artist had painted it onto canvas.

The painting seemed twelve feet high and twice that wide. After staring at it for five minutes, I walked closer and read the label.

FERNAND CORMON (1845–1924)
Cain Flying Before Jehovah's Curse
1880
Oil on canvas

The aging leader in the painting could be any number of my friends: fifty- to sixty-year-old climbers and adventurers who've spent most of their lives on foot, wandering the world's wild places.

Until reading the museum guide, the biblical story of Cain—killer of his brother Abel, son of Adam and Eve—never crossed my mind.

This painting illustrates the miserable destiny of Cain, the elder son of Adam and Eve, who after the murder of his younger brother Abel was condemned to perpetual wandering. A haggard Cain is doggedly leading his tribe.

I couldn't get the painting out of my mind. Later I read that as part of the research he did for the painting, Cormon, the artist, spent weeks in a museum outside of

Paris studying recently unearthed skeletons and stone tools, in order to know our prehistoric ancestors.

On the surface, Cormon painted the misery Cain and his family suffered after murdering his brother, Abel. But by using the most current research to depict evolutionarily correct figures to tell part of our most important creation myth, Cormon had a message for us.

Darwin had forced the question: Did God drop humans on earth fully formed and in his own image? Or are we one of the latest twigs sprouting in the outer canopy of the Tree of Life? When Darwin surmised that species evolved by natural selection in 1857 in *On the Origin of Species*, the world turned upside down, even without his directly suggesting that modern humans had been subject to those same wondrous processes. He waited until 1879 to do that with the publication of *The Descent of Man*, reigniting the controversy. Many believe that the publicity of Darwin's later book, along with the discovery of spectacular prehistoric art in a cave at Altamira in Spain, motivated Cormon to paint *Cain* to further disturb the status quo.

Do the figures in Cormon's painting represent an early, prehuman stage in the 3-billion-year history of our species, or are they *us* because God made one and only one species of man? Or—and this is my question—do Cormon's anthropologically accurate figures represent us, but only at the latest phase of our ongoing evolution, while suggesting that we've been who we currently are for an awfully long time?

Those who believed that Cormon's figures were prehuman did so because Cain and his family look markedly different than the perfect, classical Greek statue bodies.

When I found "Cain and the Problem of the Prehistoric Body," the 2002 article that art historian Martha Lucy wrote about Cormon, his painting, and the controversy surrounding it, I was sure it would help me make my argument that Cormon's characters were based on modern humans, albeit wild ones.

This didn't happen. According to Lucy's article, Cormon's painting fanned the fiery controversy Darwin started because, to many viewers, those portrayed in it didn't look like them or anyone they'd seen before and therefore must be "prehuman"—an early intermediate step in our evolutionary process between apes and humans. This implied that we came from earlier life forms rather than directly from Adam and Eve.

Martha Lucy suggests that in the painting, Cain and his family are Neanderthal.

Martha Lucy has not met my friends.

I don't think my friends are Neanderthals.

To build support for my theory that Cain and his people are modern humans, I showed the catalog with a photo of the painting to my friend Vaughn, a former climber, now a professional wilderness guide working in southeastern Utah. After years moving about in wild places, he's a bit bent over, skinny—not an ounce of fat. Wind and sun have turned his skin to leather. His wild, shoulder-length hair is turning gray. He could have been the model for Cain in Cormon's painting. Vaughn looked at the photo for a few seconds and then said, "The ape factor." He explained that to save energy older climbers walk like Cain is walking in the photo, slightly bent, arms swinging, hands low brushing knees. On seeing the painting, Vaughn never considered that the figures were ancestors from an earlier evolutionary step. Cain and his family seemed to be biologically modern humans—not all modern people, but *wild* people, people who live wild lives in the natural world, constantly experiencing and embracing natural systems.

Fifteen kilometers west of Paris, the Château de Saint-Germain-en-Laye is home to the Musée d'Archéologie Nationale. Originally a royal residence where Louis VI ("the Fat") built a fort in 1124 and Louis XIV ("the Sun King") was born in 1638, Napoleon III restored the château and installed his archaeological collections there in 1862. The building's spectacular Gothic architecture surrounded by nearly infinite grounds with dozens of statues and thousands of trees in perfect lines with perfectly leveled crowns and exploding cherry blossoms were all good reasons to visit there, but we went for the Paleolithic collection. We went to learn whether Cain is Neanderthal or one of us. According to Martha Lucy, Cormon made regular visits to this museum to study bones and artifacts in order to more accurately render people in his paintings. He carefully compared Neanderthal and Cro-Magnon characteristics, but Lucy doesn't say specifically whether Cormon ever acknowledged which group he used as models.

Cro-Magnon man is named for the cave in southwest France where his fossils were found in 1868. It is now believed that after first appearing in Africa between 200,000 and 150,000 years ago, Cro-Magnon migrated to Europe 40,000 years ago. Cro-Magnon man's bones so closely match ours that experts now refer to this early ancestor as Anatomically Modern Human.

Cro-Magnon man, then, is us.

Neanderthals lived in Europe and Asia from 300,000 until 30,000 years ago. In Europe we coexisted with Neanderthal people for 10,000 years. Recent genetic evidence suggests we mated with Neanderthals before completely replacing them. Traditionally, artists have portrayed Neanderthals as brutes—humped backs and thick necks, frequently covered with hair. These "cavemen" were often used to symbolize civilization's alternative: lesser creatures engaged in the day-to-day struggle for survival using their wits and physical brawn. They were lesser because civilization was seen as a giant leap forward that allowed us to take survival for granted. In art, Neanderthal became the ultimate symbol for "other"—bent, club-carrying slaves to their modern masters.

This makes sense only as long as we consider ourselves masters of the universe.

Half a million years ago, we—*Homo sapiens sapiens*, Anatomically Modern Human, Cro-Magnon—and Neanderthal (*Homo sapiens neanderthalensis*) had a common ancestor. With the exception that Neanderthal people are stockier, much stronger, and have thicker brows and broader noses, we are very similar, anatomically. Their tools were simpler than ours—think flakes broken from rocks by hitting them with other rocks as opposed to our carefully chipped blades. We created the wondrous art found in Altamira, Lascaux, and Chauvet. We all buried our dead.

We have more in common with Neanderthals physically than we do culturally. This doesn't make it any easier to know what Cormon intended when he painted Cain and his family.

John Gurche is one of the world's leading paleo-artists who, using his skills as both artist and scientist, reconstructs prehistoric life. I saw the reconstruction of *Australopithecus sediba* he did from a 2-million-year-old fossil in *National Geographic*. Later, I found the image of the Neanderthal man he created for the Smithsonian Institute. Surely Gurche could tell me who exactly Cormon painted.

"They are fairly muscular people, as Neanderthals undoubtedly were," he said after looking at Cormon's painting. "But I don't get a sense of the squat build that Neanderthals had. And the brow ridges just aren't there, so I'd say Cain and his people look more like powerfully built modern folks."

This was good enough for me.

Cain and his family are us, Anatomically Modern Humans, Cro-Magnon man.

But we don't all find ourselves accurately mirrored in a member of Cormon's Cain family.

Assuming that all Greeks had bodies like those depicted in their statues would be like suggesting that all of us living today look the same. We come in all shapes and sizes. Stand on a corner in a big city and look at the different body types possible in genetically identical modern humans.

Variations in the modern human body are more behavioral than genetic differences. Our bodies respond to the conditions we choose to live in—sitting more than standing, riding when we could be walking, eating grains, cookies, and cheese, drinking beer. The switch from long-distance hunting to agriculture explains why many of our bones are smaller and less robust than they once were, especially our legs.

Today very few of us are out on foot looking for food—gathering plants or hunting ancient horses and zebras and bighorn sheep and carrying them back to camp. We still could if we had to. Art Devany is considered the father of "evolutionary fitness." He believes that our health is directly proportional to the extent to which we use our bodies in the way evolution intended. To illustrate what our evolved bodies are capable of, Devany cites a historical source who watched five Indian braves chase five bison into a ten-foot-deep pit. The Indians killed the bison with spears, pulled the 2,000-pound animals out of the pit, skinned and butchered them, and hauled them back to camp.

"Wild—*adj.* wild·er, wild·est: Occurring, growing, or living in a natural state; not domesticated, cultivated, or tamed." Tamed and domesticated are not the same. Unlike cattle and horses and dogs, we've not been purpose-fully adapted genetically by selective breeding. We have, however, been changed from the wild or savage state . . . chained or harnessed. We have been tamed.

I believe that our wild or savage state still exists but is buried beneath 10,000 years of civilization.

Cormon painted our biological bodies—wild bodies adapted to a nomadic, hunting and gathering life, thriving in a still-wild world. Those wild bodies kept our species alive since we first emerged in Africa. My modern friends who spend their lives moving around on foot in wild places—exploring, carrying big loads, sleeping under the stars—may be living as close to our natural state as is possible in our civilized world. Their bodies have adapted to this lifestyle, and their bodies look like those in Cormon's painting.

The current Paleo trend is an effort to regain some of the physicality our species traded away for civilization. The theory is that exercise regimes and diets designed to duplicate the lives we evolved to live will maximize our health.

It follows that in addition to being healthier individuals, people living as closely as possible to our natural state might have more access to those same tools we've always used to guarantee the survival of our species. They might instinctively know what we should do next.

If Cain's story were a dream, how would we interpret it? Adam and Eve had a good life in the Garden of

Eden in their preknowledge state. They didn't know good from evil because in that natural, wild world, there was no good or evil. Life's wild system whirred along as the successful organisms, early humans included, adapted to constantly changing conditions, while those that didn't died or went extinct. God must have wanted Adam and Eve in that garden because they were perfectly adapted to the life they had there.

I see Eve holding a bright red apple in one hand while covering her nakedness with the other. Even though God told her not to, Eve picked the apple from the Tree of Knowledge after the devil disguised as a serpent tempted her. She took that famous bite and realized she was naked. She knew the difference between good and evil, which elevated her above all other life. Adam, wanting desperately to mate with Eve, knew that he was out of luck unless he took a bite too, and in doing so joined Eve on life's balcony, looking down on everything else. The recent discovery of Mitochondrial Eve, responsible for all modern mitochondrial DNA, makes this seem not quite so farfetched.

Until the serpent showed Eve what was possible, she might not have known there was any alternative to the garden. God, representing all that is good and right, created us along with all other life to live in a wild, natural state. The devil wanted us civilized. He led us from the garden. Christian religions call this The Fall. They believe that the choices and challenges outside of the garden were necessary in order for us to grow and progress. Some say this had practical ramifications: if God intended all unborn spirits to gain earthly bodies, surely there wasn't room in the Garden of Eden.

Cain was the first human ever to be born. He grew up a farmer, cultivating the land. His little brother, Abel, was a herder. One day, they both made offerings to the Lord: Cain, some of the produce he'd grown; and Abel, the firstborn of his flock. Cain couldn't deal with the fact that the Lord accepted Abel's offering but not his own. Crazy with jealousy, Cain lured Abel out into the field where he killed him with the jawbone of an ass.

Cain the farmer killing Abel the herdsman is symbolic of a time when agriculture began to replace hunting and gathering. I can only speculate as to what this says about how God felt about agriculture—that he cursed the soil so that Cain could never farm again before sending him off to endlessly wander the earth.

If the story of this first family in the Garden of Eden is the mythical telling of our monumental transition from nomadic hunters and gatherers to civilized farmers, then the Garden of Eden is a symbol of our prehistory and cultural transformation.

By depicting Cain and his family as he did, Cormon could have been saying that the Garden of Eden story occurred during a premodern period in our history—that we've progressed culturally and biologically since leaving the garden. Or Cormon might have considered the story of Adam, Eve, Abel, and Cain—and perhaps the entire

Bible—a story, a metaphor for the entire history of modern humans.

My father, for whom I have great respect, is committed to a more literal version of this story than I am. He believes that God created the earth in seven days—though not the twenty-four-hour days we're familiar with—culminating in Adam rising from dust and then digging out one of his own ribs to create Eve. I grew up with that story but have come to replace it with a new story of creation, one involving a different concept of time, colliding continents, exploding stars, and steamy primal ooze.

Perhaps God knew what we would do with the freedom we would have outside of the garden. He must have anticipated the problems of transforming from nomadic hunting and gathering, the life for which our bodies were designed, to agriculture, which so many anthropologists have written about—population explosions, monocultural crops, sedentary lifestyles. Does all the good and comfort and beauty we've created outside of the garden compensate for the destruction we've caused? Did God foresee our ability to rationalize evil for the right price? Perhaps the planet and the life it supports would be better off if we'd never left the garden.

I refer to God as if we're friends. I'm not sure. I believe in a higher power—one so high we humans don't have the intelligence or sufficient imagination to fully understand it. Belief carries with it a level of uncertainty. When Rio's lying on the floor at my feet, I know he's there—no need for belief. When he's not there, I believe that he's out in the sun or in the other room, but I'm not sure. I'm uncertain. If I saw him walk out the door five seconds ago, my uncertainty is less than if I haven't seen him for an hour. I believe William Williams is alive in some form and that he influences me. I have both evidence and doubt. But modern religion asks us to trade our uncertainty for afterlife benefits. In my case, I get my own planet when I give up my doubt.

The word *garden* usually refers to a piece of ground cleared then tilled and planted by someone for the purpose of cultivating vegetables or flowers. The Garden of Eden in this case is the earth as God created it, in its wild state. The garden metaphor for the wild-to-civilized transition helps my argument that Cain and his family are Cro-Magnon. Anatomically Modern Human appeared in the garden 200,000 years ago. We lived there as nomadic hunters and gatherers until we left to make the transition to agriculture and civilization, outside the garden. God created us to live in peace and abundance in His garden. The devil's goal is to control us and force us into his darkness and live throughout time with him in hell. His first step, then, was to civilize us, to lure us out of the garden.

Perhaps the original role of modern technology was to enable our growing numbers to survive the scarcity we encountered once we left the garden. Now our most serious problems are the result of taking technology far beyond what we truly need, and our insatiable appetites threaten to destroy the planet. The devil must be grinning.

Vivaldi is playing on my iPhone. I pat my MacBook Pro and thank it for all the magic it regularly performs. The Musée d'Orsay, where I first encountered *Cain*, is one of the most aesthetically pleasing buildings I've ever been in. Paris itself is hundreds of square miles of the best of what civilization has created for us. I never forget how much of what I love about the modern world couldn't exist in the garden.

In the same way that departure from the garden was irreversible—no going back permanently—the changes to the landscape we've caused by leaving are also permanent. Thank goodness that the garden still exists in places in the world unaffected by civilization, where natural systems still function as they have since the beginning of time. Still wild. For most of our civilized history, all that was left of the garden were places we hadn't yet found a use for. Then back in the late 1950s a few prophetic people began to see that modern civilization had no limits. They understood the value of wild places to remind us of where we came from, who we once were, and that without action we stand to lose any connection with our past. The result was the 1964 Wilderness Act.

We need to protect wilderness in order to have points of reference—places like those where our species was born, landscapes where natural systems are still intact and functioning. Examples of the Creation. Wild places.

Freud called this wild part of ourselves the Id. He believed that in order for society to function, these wild tendencies must be repressed. Freud believed that this "cauldron of seething excitation," containing basic drives, lacking judgment, value, and morality, with complete absence of good or evil, was the source of everything wrong with civilization.

But by suppressing, repressing the Id—our *wild* tendencies—we may also be shutting ourselves off from that part of our biological *evolutionary body* containing the tools we've used to save our individual and collective selves, over and over again, throughout our entire history.

This could be why we now find ourselves in trouble.

This is not the first time in our long history that we've had a close call, but it will be the first time we've brought it on ourselves.

Hope, for me, would be to blow the dust off and clear the cobwebs away from those old, wild tools. We could combine them with the same knowledge and experience we've used to survive in numbers far beyond the earth's actual carrying capacity. We could use these ancient vital tools with the modern technologies to build a new future. How soon can we start?

Putting this genie back in the bottle—going back to the garden—isn't an option for the 7 billion of us alive today. But for those of us who know wildness and what it has always meant to our species, the garden is anywhere wild where natural systems still function, where the life force still moves boldly toward the future. Wildness flows in our veins, contains the contents of our cells, connects our muscles to our bones. It is stronger than the gravity keeping us from floating away.

Wildness is an invisible force we take for granted.

Wilderness is where we're best able to feel and taste and hear the wildness alive inside us.

Some day in the future our descendants will look back and thank us for saving some wilderness while wondering why we didn't save more. They will have survived the most recent close call and will know the role that wildness played. By then, people spending time in wilderness will be valued for the wisdom they find there. Wilderness guides like Vaughn will be hired not just by individuals looking for a meaningful vacation but by corporate leaders, government officials, academics, artists, theologians seeking answers to that unceasing evolutionary question: How do we adapt?

And Cain? I don't believe that God sent him to wander the world aimlessly. What a waste that would have been. Perhaps he's still out there with his family, just like in Cormon's painting, exploring what remains of the garden and telling stories of what is found there. Maybe we've seen him. Maybe we know him, that feeling of wild impatience moving inside.

" Wildness cannot survive becoming popular

NINE

Recapture Creek, Utah

On a cool morning in early April I was part of a group gathered in the middle of a gravel pit, east of Blanding, Utah. I prefer to be alone but I felt lucky and happy just to be out.

There were twelve of us. The General and five others rode horses. We think he is actually a general. We think he had a long career in the Defense Department in Washington, D.C., before returning home to San Juan County where he was elected to the County Commission. We would never ask him directly. We call him the General but not to his face. I was there representing SUWA, an "interested party" in the Section 106 Consultation Process required of the Bureau of Land Management by the National Historic Preservation Act to determine whether giving San Juan County a right of way to construct a road in Recapture Creek would impact the antiquities found therein.

Actually, a road already existed in Recapture Creek. It was built secretly and illegally in 2006. This act precipitated the BLM closing the canyon in order to protect the significant archaeological resources existing there—the hundreds of prehistoric Native American sites that have been identified by government archaeologists and the thousands that haven't. Evidence shows that the closer an archaeological site is to a road, the more likely it is to be vandalized.

Fortunately, I wasn't needed at the meetings, only on the field trip. Rio and William were with me. We'd come down the night before and camped on a sandstone bluff between juniper trees.

"Well, just last week we crammed another nice ninety-minute meeting into a full day," the General had answered when asked about how the process was going. He seemed in a good mood, considering how complicated he thought the federal government was making this issue, and most everything else he and his fellow commissioners were elected to deal with. I'd never before seen him in a good mood, but then I'd never been with him outside. Obviously there is more to the General than he reveals to those of us he considers his enemies.

"How's Brooke?" he said, surprising me. "Great day for a ride, isn't it?" Besides the mandatory nod, the General had only spoken directly to me once before.

A month earlier I was in Monticello for the Monday-morning commission meeting. At SUWA we like to go to these meetings as often as possible to see if wilderness gets mentioned. The meetings always begin with prayer, which I take it—from the careful wording Bruce, the chairman, uses—has been quite controversial in the past. "We like to begin our meetings with a word of prayer, an inspirational thought, or a moment of silence." I swear he uses the exact language each time, as if the San Juan County district attorney wrote it. Nine times out of ten, a man, usually a county employee, sends out a signal that he'd volunteer, as if they take turns. I go to fewer than half of the meetings and have never heard a woman pray. Only once have I heard anything but a traditional Mormon prayer, and that was when Ken, the third commissioner, a Navajo Indian, gave the most beautiful prayer in his native language. A large part of the Navajo Nation overlaps San Juan County, and as a result they always have the votes to make one of their own a commissioner. I've yet to experience the moment of silence option.

One morning I surprised everyone when I stood up. "I'll pray," I said. When I introduced myself, including that I worked for SUWA, a tangible hush spread out in the room. They hate SUWA. They think SUWA wants them all to move away so their entire county can be designated Wilderness. The General turned toward me and asked with a huge grin, "And which God will you be praying to?" That was the only other time he'd spoken to me directly. I channeled my great, great-grandfather, Brigham Young, praying for continued guidance for the leaders and to be reminded that, regardless of which side of the political spectrum we're on, we all share more than we don't. I "Amen-ed" and sat down.

The General surprised me again with his spurs. I'd

never seen anything like them, but then I don't know much about horses. I don't ride horses. I love them and would never use them for my own entertainment or to carry me just because I didn't want to walk. I know that inside those deep large eyes there is something very mysterious and good. I know a number of men whose first wives were in love with horses. I don't know a cowboy who either doesn't seriously limp or isn't bent over from too many falls from too many horses. I don't ever want a horse.

The spurs worn by the General were not the typical small, spiked wheels connected to a cowboy boot via a u-shaped silver bracket, designed to hurt a horse into doing the will of its rider. The General's spurs were a broad, blunt piece of smooth metal designed to less painfully nudge a horse in a particular direction. This surprised me.

This surprised me because it showed the General to have a sensitive side, a side with which I was not familiar. Most of my interactions with him involved him experimenting with the amount of intimidation and pain he could inflict upon anyone who didn't agree with him. I always sensed it was a game with him. I've felt differently about him since.

Once the group had gathered, as if by some invisible signal those on horseback dropped off the back of the flat, quarried area onto a well-established trail. Those of us on foot—Rose Chilcot from Great Old Broads for Wilderness and I, representing the environmental community; the Bureau of Land Management staff, including the field office manager; specialists from the National Historic Preservation Office; and a number of private archaeologists—followed, so as not to slow the horse people down. The General's wife was the only woman on a horse.

Rio was on his own, which was a mistake. Attracted by some seductive, ancient smell, he snuck into a ruin and started digging in a far corner. A huge no-no. The BLM officials, dog lovers though they were, freaked out. I swear Rio smiled as I connected him to his leash.

Recapture Creek has the basic features that have had a magnetic pull on me since my first experience in the Escalante area in the early 1970s: vertical sandstone walls separated by a wild stream; lush willows and tall grasses; ageless cottonwoods; canyon wrens, turkey vultures, a kinglet, a raven; coyote and deer tracks; dragonflies; evidence that between A.D. 100 and 900 this was home to thousands—people giving birth, bringing dead deer and bighorn sheep and rice grass and herbs in from the margins, making functional art, burying their dead.

We hadn't walked five minutes when the BLM archaeologist pointed out evidence of those who once called this canyon home. Stacked stone walls along the cliff base. Granaries. Habitation sites and rooms with views. I'd been in this canyon before and had seen evidence of the Ancient Ancestors of the Pueblo People (the new name for Anasazi), but that was only a fraction of what I saw then through the trained eyes of experienced archaeologists. They pointed out the difference between piles: stones from fallen walls and rocks randomly placed by time. They alerted us to all-but-invisible dwellings high in cliff niches and a point in the canyon where the culprit road builders had exposed human remains with their machinery. The archaeologists seemed to see the canyon through the eyes of those who had lived out lives there a thousand years before.

The walkers caught up with the horse people taking a break in the canyon bottom. The BLM archaeologist was unable to contain his passion for this ancient culture in general and for Recapture Canyon in particular. Telling a story, he breathed life into the small, open area where we gathered. When he crouched beside what seemed to be a random pile of rocks, we watched it become a fire pit. Suddenly people dressed in feathers and wearing masks danced in my imagination. I could swear I heard drums. The horse riders were skeptical and frustrated. They shrugged and muttered. It wasn't that they didn't believe what the archaeologist was telling them but that they couldn't see the significance.

"How many piles of rocks like this one do we need?" the General asked the archaeologist. In other words, why is all this archaeological evidence necessary? Haven't we learned already what we can from it?

We politely ate lunch and made small talk about each other's kids, and they talked about a recent storm and their cows. No one mentioned Barack Obama or Dr. Redd.

Dr. Redd is James Redd, who had delivered many of the babies born in San Juan County and took care of anyone in need. He committed suicide months earlier. He was depressed after being pulled from his Blanding home as part of an elaborate FBI predawn sting. He was arrested along with twenty-three others for desecrating ancient graves for artifacts they took and then sold at exorbitant prices to an undercover agent.

The election of President Obama somehow signaled the end of everything these people hold dear. He did not disappoint them. Within months of his inauguration a list of potential national monuments was leaked to the press. People in rural Utah hate national monuments. Cedar Mesa, an area so rich in cultural resources many consider it a 50,000-acre outdoor museum, was on that list. Nowhere on earth is this wealth of human history so accessible and so brilliant. And rarely can the descendants of those living in a place 1,000 years ago be found still practicing similar ways of life, which is why it needs monument designation and the budgets for protection and research that come with it. Within an hour of the list being discussed on NPR, rumors began circulating—"Obama is closing Cedar Mesa"—and phones began ringing at local guide services and guesthouses, with people from throughout the country calling to come visit.

While I was eating and listening, a species of dragonfly known as the variegated meadowhawk landed in a giant skunkbush near where I sat against a rock. Years ago, during a daydream, I found a granite stone engraved with a black dragonfly in the bottom of a green metal World War II ammo can. The occurrence of this dream roughly coincided with discovering William Williams. Earlier that summer I had taken on the task of learning the names and natural histories of those dragonflies I've been able to observe. This meadowhawk had just returned from a quick hunting foray with a nearly invisible gnat to finish chewing and swallow. I made mental notes regarding its size, the spots on its thorax, its intricate red-and-black patterned abdomen like a cowboy's leather lariat.

Perhaps it is the serious nature of this trip that forced me to think logically about my relationship with dragonflies. I was there with professionals and officials trying to focus on the technical and legal aspects of a right of way in this canyon with respect to the National Historic Preservation Act. Instead of making notes to formulate into future arguments, I was busy interpreting the communications the dragonfly brought me from the inner world.

To many Native Americans, dragonflies are the souls of the dead, delivering messages between worlds. I've learned that if I'm open to worlds beyond the obvious and comfortable in the symbolic and mythological realms, these stunning creatures can play an active role in my life. Although I don't—and probably can't—understand the exact mechanism, I trust that noticing a dragonfly indicates that something important for me to know about is going on in the lower, inner world.

There in Recapture, the lower, inner world may have been directly beneath my feet.

Thousands of Anasazi people must be buried in that canyon. Archaeologists can estimate both the numbers of people who lived here at any one time and the amount of time it was occupied. Dr. Redd's recent sting greatly intensifies the issue. This bust wasn't the first, and based on the prices artifacts bring at illegal markets, it won't be the last, especially if roads continue to exist in places like Recapture Canyon.

"Pot hunting" is part of the San Juan County culture. Back in the mid-1990s, some of the same people went on trial for desecrating a corpse. They were rummaging a gravesite for the artifacts that these ancient people buried with their dead to ease the transition to the next life. As I recall, the culprits were exonerated because of their attorney's ability to convince the judge and jury that the bones in question weren't actually part of a burial site because ancient people didn't always bury their dead, that "their bones are scattered all over this country." In other words, good people like those being accused of grave desecration considered those buried in these graves to be different, somehow: other.

The day Dr. Redd breathed carbon monoxide through a hose he'd connected to the tailpipe of his Jeep, I heard a radio interview with Forrest Cuch, a member of the Ute tribe who at the time directed Utah's Department of Indian Affairs. He said, "American Indians are human beings, too." Then Cuch struck a main nerve in me when he suggested that people who disturb the graves of other people "suffer from a lack of consciousness."

Hearing Mr. Cuch say something I'd been thinking myself but hadn't the nerve to say surprised and shocked me. While he specifically targeted those accused of actually breaking known laws, I think the term applies to an entire faction of people who have arrived at the conclusion that they are somehow God's chosen. That any efforts to give proper standing to people of different races or sexual identity or, God forbid, different species, is not only a waste of time and money but threatens our fragile and improbable stature.

Although there are few things we agree on, I have a great deal of respect for the General. I know he's very intelligent and well read, and I would bet that he's a stalwart leader in his local Mormon ward. Having attended numerous County Commission meetings, I know that he was extremely upset with how the FBI handled the arrests of his Blanding neighbors and friends. He's been very clear in his disgust over the closing of the road in Recapture and the fact that the ability of his neighbors and friends to ride their ATVs there trumps any damage to Native American graves that might occur as a result. I would bet that the General believes that gay people should not be able to marry each other, and if he believes the climate is warming, it has nothing to do with modern humans. Or that evolution has anything to do with how we got here. If I had to guess, to the General, nature is first a source of the commodities we have been blessed with to fuel and feed our ever-expanding population, and second a place for recreation. I realize I might be wrong about some or all of this. I'd never ask.

Part of getting older is becoming comfortable with knowing that arguments aren't worth having unless they might move those arguing closer together rather than farther apart. Although it is frustrating, knowing that no argument I can make will convince the General to abandon his position on a road through Recapture Canyon, it is also a relief. The General is so confident, so imposing, that he would probably laugh at me for believing in the strength and value of an inner world—that dragonflies carried messages from that world to this one.

Liberals are often so politically correct that we can't speak publically about this expanding difference between what appears to be the same two sides to every issue. This has nothing to do with intelligence or experience, only the breadth and depth of the information we choose to pursue.

On good days, I think we're making progress on the Wilderness issue in San Juan County—that a reasonable compromise might be possible. On bad days, I don't. The bad days outnumber the good.

Compromise means that two different sides are points on a line and somewhere along that line between them is a magical place where a correct answer lives. Protecting wilderness is not about specific places and numbers of acres. It is not really about roads and motors and where to dig and drill and cut and where not to. Protecting wilderness is based on wholeness—complete and functioning natural systems, where life spins and whirls—movement that we can see and be part of and then be moved by. This is more complicated than points along an imagined line. And it's not just wilderness where this is a factor, but in everything that matters. I think that this line is stretching and growing, the different ends further and further apart, and even halfway along it, right smack in the middle, is unacceptable to everyone and anyone who cares.

After thinking about what Mr. Cuch said, and being excited that someone had the nerve to say it, I realized that I was taking for granted what the term *consciousness* actually means. Lately, while looking in all directions for some sign that we might actually survive—turn the corner on this climate crisis and the impending doom associated with it—the idea of an evolution of consciousness comes up. Perhaps the same lack of consciousness that would allow one person to raid the grave of another might also allow someone to feel superior to a person of another race or gender or sexual orientation. Should we make consciousness a factor in arguments over endangered species, global warming, open space, and wilderness?

I read books and articles on consciousness. I wrote a few paragraphs as background and then sent it with some questions about consciousness to people who might help me. I sent it to a writer, an editor of books on consciousness, a follower of an East Indian teacher, a yoga teacher, and a philosopher. The information I asked for came back so quickly and in such bundles that at first I wasn't sure what to make of it. Then I came up with something.

"Consciousness" is either core consciousness or extended consciousness. All humans have the former, as do some higher-order animals. Having core consciousness means we are aware that we are alive. It is biological and, therefore, a tool for survival. Simple.

I feel safe in saying that the terms *consciousness* and *wholeness* are related. Jung's idea of individuation or wholeness seems to fit: that the goal of life is to discover our complete, whole, self, which is made up of both the conscious (the day-to-day, the obvious and tangible) and unconscious (the stuff of dreams and the source for imagination). Jung believed that bringing the unconscious out of the deep dark recesses into the light was necessary to becoming whole and individuated. This may mean that only those who are less whole would ravage the graves of other people; only less whole people assume that they—and only they—are God's chosen.

Psychological health may be based on this idea of wholeness, that level to which we're able to integrate the conscious, outer world with the inner world of the unconscious.

The inner and outer, unconscious and conscious worlds. Dragonflies are navigating between them, delivering messages from one to the other.

Could the "lack of consciousness" to which Cuch referred be the lack of one's ability or desire to accept both worlds?

As I understand it, divine or extended consciousness relates to Jung's idea of the collective unconscious, which many believe contains the entire evolutionary history of our species, going back to those first one-celled organisms floating together in that primal soup. Clearly, consciousness is not something we can create or learn but is something to which we all have access. If that's true, then an "evolution of consciousness" may be as simple as tapping more deeply into this driving force, which from the ultimate beginning has been responsible for passing life onto the future.

I didn't get completely comfortable with all this until I made a picture. At the center of the page, I drew consciousness as a green blob. I colored the rest of the page blue and called it unconsciousness. The green blob has a mouth—an opening with which it takes bites from the unconscious and is nourished and grows. Unconsciousness is food for consciousness. Consciousness grows in proportion to the amount of unconsciousness it eats. There is much more unconscious than we will ever need; we will never run out of it.

Those who would desecrate the graves of others, train dogs to kill each other for sport, own slaves, or who see hatred as a skill do not know that unconsciousness is food. Their green blob with the mouth does not grow much because it eats other, less nourishing food. It is in danger because the other food is only available in diminishing quantities. Perhaps they have placed a taboo on eating the unlimited unconsciousness in the same way that the Greenland Norse may have had a taboo against eating the fish to which they had unlimited access, a taboo that led to their eventual demise.

I was feeling as if I'd tapped into something and began making a chart defining different levels of consciousness according to different forms of prejudice. (Are those who think men are the superior gender at a higher or lower level of consciousness than those who believe modern Americans are the chosen people?)

I was thinking about that chart in Recapture that day when we stopped to marvel at a beautiful white atlatl point. Standing in part of the canyon where the walls seemed more distant from each other than they had previously and the sun coming down, burning my neck for the first time all year, it struck me: this is the same hierarchical thinking that has gotten us into this mess. This thinking was from the outer world. I'm sure the Dalai Lama or Gandhi wouldn't put people into categories, one on top of another, according to the quality of their consciousness. My mind had given me an elevated position to feed my ego. Fabricating this hierarchy is a demonstration of my own lack of consciousness. Shit. When would I ever learn?

With the new spring and dragonflies once again bringing me messages, I hoped I was back to believing in my personal green blob and knowing that it grows only when I'm being aware, paying the closest possible attention to each moment, by "eating" unconsciousness, absorbing it and the universe, partaking of a billion years of wisdom.

The General and his horse people were long gone when the rest of us crossed Recapture Creek for the last time. We pushed our way through healthy forests of willows where small birds fluttered and up onto an old road. A large insect rubbed its legs together while sitting in a distant tree, creating a sound like a toy noisemaker.

We were all tired but happy as we moved toward the vehicles we could see in the distance. I wasn't sure how far we walked that day, but miles don't matter as much as real movement.

The Blanding raids resulted in a number of convictions, fines, no time actually served, and two more suicides in addition to Dr. Redd, including that of the FBI informant.

Without warning, Forrest Cuch and two state archaeologists were fired and escorted from their offices by security guards for doing what they thought was their job: protecting the state's cultural resources. Cuch's statements on the Blanding raids likely contributed to his undoing.

Two Blanding men were tried and convicted of the 2006 building of the illegal ATV trail in Recapture—the misdemeanor of damaging property under the jurisdiction of the Bureau of Land Management. The judge fined them $35,000 and probation, saying that "it was not possible to attribute all the damage in the canyon to these two men."

The General, knowing his time as commissioner was short due to term limits, picked his successor, a young conservative Blanding accountant named Phil Lyman. The actual election was merely a formality. The General now serves on Utah's Balanced Resource Committee.

Phil Lyman led a group of "rebels" on motorized ATVs on a protest ride through Recapture Canyon. Among the riders was Ryan Bundy, the son of Cliven Bundy, a Nevada rancher who earlier had made national news when a group of armed militants joined him to protest the BLM's insistence that he pay the million dollars he owed in unpaid grazing fees.

Lyman and four others were indicted for their illegal actions in Recapture Canyon. Lyman was sentenced to ten days in jail and probation.

The General, in the *Salt Lake Tribune*, criticized

Bundy

RECAPTURE CREEK, UTAH ◆ 163

the ride as an "illegal gesture that would only set back the county's desire to open up the canyon just east of Blanding."

And early in 2016, Ryan Bundy was injured during a shootout with authorities on a remote Oregon highway. He and his brother Ammon led the takeover of the Malheur National Wildlife Refuge by a group of cowboys believing that the federal government has no right to own western lands. To date, sixteen, including the Bundy brothers, have been indicted. One, LaVoy Finnicum, was killed during the shootout in which Bundy was injured.

TEN

Dead Horse Point, Utah

Lately, Wilderness designations are difficult to come by. The idea of wilderness has been divided up along party lines like everything else. Designations that are made come only after years of dialogue, process, negotiation, and ultimately compromise. The resulting legislation often contains language antithetical to wildness and creates Wilderness that the authors of the 1964 Wilderness Act might not recognize. The process breaks down when the two sides are so far apart on specific elements of potential legislation that any point midway between them is unacceptable to both. The president of the United States can then protect a wild landscape by creating a national monument using the authority given him by the 1906 Antiquities Act. There is a strong tradition for this, and many of our most cherished national parks began as national monuments with the stroke of the presidential pen. In 1996, after the failure of the last in a series of efforts by the Utah state government to once and for all settle the wilderness debate, President Clinton designated the Grand Staircase–Escalante National Monument. A favorite photo of mine was taken that day of the president standing with one arm around Terry and the other around Mike Matz, SUWA's then executive director.

SUWA originally hired me for one year to represent them in two county Wilderness processes. Only when those broke down and both sides acknowledged that any reasonable compromise was impossible was I able to extend my SUWA career into the field, ground-truthing maps. The end of those county processes—in San Juan and Emery Counties—marked the beginning of efforts by the entire community of Utah wilderness advocates to promote Greater Canyonlands National Monument.

The idea for Canyonlands National Park can be traced back to a 1936 map entitled *Escalante National Monument.* Harold Ickes, secretary of the interior in Franklin Roosevelt's administration, proposed that a 7,000-square-mile area spanning from what is now I-70 on the north to the San Juan River on the south be protected for its wild values. In 1964, after decades of political maneuvering, economic analysis, ranting, raving, the 515 square miles (or 330,000 acres) which remained of that original map was officially declared Canyonlands National Park. Recently, park officials have proposed that the park be completed—expanded to its ecological boundaries. Conservation organizations believe the most effective way to do that is to convince President Barack Obama to designate a national monument on wild lands adjacent to the existing national park. SUWA played a key role in developing one of a number of proposals.

An early part of our strategy involved a meeting with the Utah director of the Bureau of Land Management, which had jurisdiction over the lands in the proposal. We met in a Moab office, where we showed him maps and answered questions. Then we drove together to Dead Horse Point.

While officially a state park, Dead Horse Point has the best, most accessible view of the Greater Canyonlands area. Its name comes from the wild horses who died of thirst there after some brain-dead cowboys thought they'd found the perfect corral—a plateau perched on top of 2,000-foot cliffs, with only a narrow neck of thirty yards that required fencing.

We all talked and pointed, oohed and aahed, and then I wandered off toward one of the overlooks. I was leaning up against the stone wall built to keep us from falling thousands of feet to our deaths, taking in the massive view. A woman stood to my left, between me and the educational sign describing the geological epochs associated with the rock layers that could be seen from that vantage. We stood quietly for a few minutes before I began wondering if she was okay. She seemed to be in a trance. She stared out toward the horizon without moving—not blinking, not turning her head or shifting her weight. I couldn't tell if she was breathing. I didn't know what to do, thinking she might be having a seizure. I waited another minute before deciding against waving my hand in front of her eyes, and spoke to her instead.

"Incredible view, isn't it?"

Without turning her head to see who'd just spoken to her, she added words to what she'd obviously been thinking.

"I can see it," she said. "I can finally see forever."

She said "forever" as if it were something real, a thing, a noun and not the adverb it usually is, meaning endless or continual time. The way she said "forever" changed the way I think about the future. Sure, she may have been referring only to the view and the immense distance. But it is possible that she was having an epiphany about time. Seeing 300 million years of time defined by the exposed rock layers stretching out before her may have freed up her mind in a way that allowed her to see further into the future than ever before. Below her, the Colorado River was still cutting down through those layers, something it began 150 million years before. This may have connected her to a much deeper past. Seeing new, vast distances back into the past and forward into the future created a new definition of forever: the full spectrum of time.

I wondered if many of the ecological and social problems we face today are rooted in how we personally interpret the word *forever.*

The woman kept staring, and I joined my group as they pointed out different landscape features and where the monument boundary might be that makes the most geographical sense. I tried engaging in the conversation, but my mind centered on "forever." Suddenly, as if William Williams was there whispering in my ear, I heard, "Your ability to see 'forever' might be related to how far back in the past you're willing to look." That was the importance of the woman in the trance. Perhaps the length of the past equals the length of the future.

A recent news report on just how polarized we've become as a country included an on-camera interview with a woman in Tennessee who believed that Christ's second coming is just around the corner, that the world as we know it will soon end. She also told the interviewer that God created the earth in seven days. Short past. Short future. I doubt this woman has been to the edge of that cliff at Dead Horse Point. Half of the U.S. Congress is supported by the religious right, many of whom are convinced that biblical evidence shows that the end is near—that the worst of what we see almost daily in the news, the earthquakes, hurricanes, famine, wars, can all be found in Revelation as signs of the apocalypse. Short future. They insist that evolution is only a theory and should be taught as such in public schools. They believe in creationism or intelligent design, the idea that the earth was created in seven days or 7,000 years and not the billions of years that scientists acknowledge. Short past.

At least there is an explanation for current public policy that seems determined to expedite the unraveling of many of the natural systems on which our survival depends. Extracting the last of our resources, polluting the air, watching species go extinct at rates the earth has never seen only makes sense if we know that life is coming to an end before it's all used up.

Of course, those making decisions for big business would see this all as an asset, a bottom-line benefit that minimizes costs associated with caring about any future beyond the next quarter's earnings reports. I don't think that those in control of corporate America all believe that we are in end-times, but if end-times were a factor in the congressional vote to allow drilling for oil in the Arctic National Wildlife Refuge, if end-times have anything to do with pressure to frack and drill my beloved red rock wilderness in Southern Utah, and if laws supporting clean air, protecting us from mercury and other toxins are being overturned, canceled, or castrated into uselessness because of this end-time philosophy, then end-times means profit. This is of particular concern during a time when corporations are considered people in financing campaigns, even though alternatives exist demonstrating that businesses no longer need to suffer to protect the environment.

I'm sure that all these people think they're right. I would hope that any one of them alone might do some serious soul-searching and back off even a bit to ask the question, "What if I'm wrong?" and think twice before making life-threatening decisions. Now corporations seriously influence political decisions that undermine or eliminate environmental protections or human rights legislation. Meanwhile, scientists, scholars, thinkers, artists are caught with all the information to set things straight but without the language or the money required to make sense to those in charge.

The only way I can get out of bed in the morning is to keep looking for the root cause, hoping to see how it is that we've strayed so much from the path our species has been on for millions of years. "We the People" may be divided based on our personal relationship with time. We're all living in the personal, a self-absorbed place where we never acknowledge that life will go on after our deaths. Some of us include family and extended family, possibly even dead family as part of our past and future. We see personal history beginning with the earliest direct ancestor whose name is known or can be found on the Mormon Church's *Family Search* website. Others live as part of the Family of Man, ours being the most recent generation of the species, *Homo sapiens*. And some of us live believing we are part of all life, going back to the first one-celled organisms moving tentatively in those early warm seas.

Some of us are able to think our way into a personal biological context and begin to see ourselves as individual members of a species. This means getting beyond the idea that the name *Homo sapiens* applies only to the bones that anthropologists like Richard Leakey are lucky to find in

Africa once in a while. William Williams appeared on the far edge of my genealogy chart, implying that he was among my first ancestors—the seeds of my family tree. Meeting him linked me to Charles Darwin, who through his work connected me across time to all life. William Williams has become living tissue, the small twig connecting my family to the tree of life, splicing genealogy to biology.

Modernity cannot completely squelch our animalness. If we not only understood but also believed what most anthropological information suggests—that we first appeared on the African savannah over 200,000 years ago—we might also be able to consider the idea that our future, the idea of *forever*, stretches over the same vast time frame.

And I believe that it is possible, accurate, and ultimately responsible to feel personally a part of all life going back 3 billion years to the beginning of beginnings, to a steamy place that still has the scientists wondering. Believing in the deepest personal past makes it possible to imagine an infinite future, endless hope, and confidence that the same natural systems that got us here will continue. In this case, forever is a very long time.

Separating from this deep past is the only way we've allowed ourselves to create and contribute to situations that threaten the long future. Real solutions may require that we reconnect to deep and distant time.

I'll begin with two personal assumptions:

First, I believe that regardless of the deteriorating state of the earth, wars, hunger, and inhumanity, most people think they're doing what's right as opposed to what's wrong. This is difficult to imagine. I know that there are exceptions to this.

Second, I believe that there is an underlying goodness, rightness, and order to the universe. Call it what you will—God, a higher power, Great Spirit, Yahweh, Allah—but something is out there holding this all together, and it is big, complex, and beyond the most distant and radical limits of our ability to understand or even imagine, which renders meaningless all the arguments we have about life and death and what's out there beyond the beyond. However incomprehensible this energy is, it not only makes all life possible but provides everything life needs to flourish.

I feel good knowing that something is true even when it is beyond my ability to know. Once, I had to "know" everything, or at least act like I did. We felt pressure as children on Sunday to stand in front of the congregation and say "I know the Church is true" or "I know that God lives and answers my prayers." Writing it now reminds me of all the mantras we grew up with. As I grew older, I felt a different pressure—to replace knowledge that no longer served me with new knowledge, a pressure that at times threatened my sanity. William helped me with this. "Knowing" he was real, but in some un-known form or sense, became a kind of freedom. Freedom from knowing. Freedom to not know. Freedom to wonder.

All this was going through my head as we began walking back to the cars. The paved trail leading to the parking lot was more crowded than before. I chuckled to myself, excited about all the people on their way to see "forever" and how hopeful that was. I turned to see if the woman was still staring, but she was gone.

SUWA eventually joined forces with other conservation organizations and twenty-three Native American tribes in a proposal to President Obama to create a national monument adjacent to Canyonlands National Park. On December 28, 2016, after two years of public meetings and private negotiations and threatening rhetoric from Utah's political establishment, President Obama signed the law establishing the Bears Ears National Monument, named for a pair of iconic plateaus south of the existing park. This monument will protect 1.35 million acres of land considered sacred to Native people.

The beautifully written proclamation reads: "From earth to sky, the region is unsurpassed in wonders. The star-filled nights and natural quiet of the Bears Ears area transport visitors to an earlier eon. Against an absolutely black night sky, our galaxy and others more distant leap into view."

For many, this monument represents a great healing for past injustices.

ELEVEN

Three Crossings, Wyoming

William didn't just drop dead. Years later, his son John George, who was with him when he died, wrote in his journal, "When we reached Laramie my father took sick with Mountain Fever." He was referring to Fort Laramie, a major military fort and resupply point along the Mormon Trail, over 150 miles east of Three Crossings. "Mountain Fever" was likely typhoid fever, a disease that flourishes in unsanitary conditions. Averaging sixteen miles per day, William must have laid in the back of their wagon for ten days, suffering from intense muscular pain, abdominal cramping, dehydration, and mental confusion.

Ten days he lay back there, in and out of dreams, I imagine. John George was at the reins, with Mary a constant presence by William's side, cooling him off as best she could with a soaked rag.

In those dreams, he sometimes found himself looking up from a deep, dark cellar toward a faint light. During those dreams he saw birds sitting on tree branches silhouetted against that light or insects strung together in descending size, flying in long strands toward the source of the light. Or the dogs he'd been walking with for weeks, sitting, waiting for him. During some of those dreams he followed the birds or the dogs or the insects back home where he floated invisibly through the neighborhood. At times, fevered, half in, half out, he would talk out loud to no one about those friends he saw, their long dark capes, how slowly they moved, and how they'd all learned a new language. Mary, sitting by his side, would laugh out loud. Even with her own internal pressures constantly building as the eagerness with which her family left England turned to anxiousness, which turned to fear when William became sick, and at times exploded into dread, she would laugh at the worlds to which William's fever transported him. "If he's out of his mind," she'd ask herself, "where is he?"

When he was lucid, William was angry. He was too weak to lift his head to look out from the wagon at where they'd been or who was following. He would spend daylight hours guessing from the shape of the shadow their feet made exactly which insects or birds stood above him on the white canvas. Most of the birds were lazy ravens, he thought, riding along camp to camp. He believed he could estimate speed and distance covered based on the regular squeaks of the left rear wheel and the movement of the spot of light on the flat surface of their wooden chest, from the sunbeam coming through a pinhole above him.

He was angry because he wanted to walk across America.

Rio and I are camped near a lone tree at the base of the Rattlesnake Cliffs, a giant granite outcropping a few miles east of Jeffrey City, Wyoming. These giant rocks—their shape and size in this evening light—could be the scene of a fascinating fairy tale in which good and bad monsters battle for the souls of young travelers. If I wait long enough, the side of one giant rock might slide open, exposing a science fiction city on a distant planet, its intergalactic spaceships poised to launch on a journey to destroy the earth. Although still living, this huge conifer has sacrificed its lower branches to the woodpile next to me, fuel for many fires. Rio is off exploring. The summer sun is low, and the air is gold and cooler than I deserve. The vibration I hear could be the complete absence of sound or the scraping together of the minute pebbles a thousand ants are clearing from the entrance to their mound. Or it could be the buzz and crackle of all the organisms working in the factory time has made from the dead horse in the clearing above me, where death is being turned back into life. Although this old camp I've found at the base of these rocks is only a few feet higher than the broad plains of sage and blackbrush, I feel as if I am seeing forever. Buried pipelines carrying natural gas frequently rise to the surface out in front of me. Remnants of an old uranium mill can be found nearby, and

I've heard talk of reopening mines. The land has been grazed and grazed again. I see antelope to the south and six horses to the west—all wild—periodically lifting their heads from the bright grass to face the red sun. A marsh hawk flutters above the sage, its white rump glowing in the morning light.

I know from journal entries and maps that William Williams died nearby. But I also know this from the intangible story lodged between boulders and caught in fences, spread atom by atom from the soil through grasses and leafy herbs into the ants and deer and birds. Stories, I'm now certain, live as long as they are told and die only when forgotten. I know now that stories can be resurrected. William's once entirely forgotten story came back to life the moment I started uncovering it. At first I was arrogant enough to believe that I had the power to bring to life any ancestor whose story I decided to pursue. But the further I traveled—the further I fell—the more obvious it became that this story needed to live and came after me, hunted me and haunts me still. I became the host, the messenger, the one to deliver it across that difficult divide separating the inner ancient world, where truth and reality and our entire evolutionary history are stored, and the outer world, where our arrogant struggles with meaning and worth threaten to destroy us along with this wonder-bread world we've created. I have no proof, only impressions I can't explain coming at dawn when I'm neither asleep nor awake, ideas like foreign words that for some magical reason or purpose I understand. Or a subtle pressure, the size and weight of a hand, turning me toward something I might have missed, nudging me forward into the dark, or just resting quietly on my shoulder.

Rio has been gone long enough to worry me, so dragging my old stiff body off my lawn chair, I wander up the small canyon behind me, thinking I'll find him chewing on that dead horse. I find a good path, which, along with dried cow pies, suggests that these cliffs provide welcome summer shade. Time slows as the light dims and invisible insects begin to hum. Rio surprises me from behind just as I get to the huge carcass. The horse has been dead too long even for Rio, who sniffs around its edges but has no interest in a piece of hide or a bone to chew or in entering the tent-cavern formed by its cape draped over elegantly curved ribs. The flies and maggots are nearly through with this horse. The hide is thick and hard and unbending, more hoof than flesh, a protective shell. In a week or a month, the tendons and cartilage will disintegrate, collapsing the last of this animal into itself. In a year what hasn't been dragged away the soil will have absorbed.

I think of William's body, not far from here. From journals I know that when he died, he was wrapped in a blanket, placed in a quick hole dug for him, and covered with the tailgate from his wagon "to hold the dirt from covering his body." I'd read stories about other Mormon pioneers who died during a freak winter storm and were buried at Martin's Cove, a few miles east of here. As they

moved on the next day, those who survived recalled seeing hungry wolves pull the buried bodies from their shal-
low graves and drag them away.

Wolves might have dragged William to a safe place
and torn his flesh and muscles from his bones while ravens waited. When the wolves were finished, the ravens
swooped in and ate the small pieces still clinging to the
bones and plucked out William's eyes. The turkey vultures came once the corpse began rotting. When all the
tissue was gone, bones were all that was left of William,
the edges of which small rodents chewed for calcium that
would help them through the coming winter.

Or, should William have been buried deep and se-
cure enough beneath that stone-weighted tailgate, that
ample dirt, something else happened. Entirely different
animals found him attractive at different stages.

William's own bacteria, present before his death,
began consuming him from the inside. These bacteria fed
on his body while flies drank the fluids oozing from him,
his tissues being too acidic. The bacteria and excrement
from the fly larvae—the maggots—neutralized the acid,
turning William nearly to liquid, making him attractive
to blowflies and flesh flies. Beetles found his corpse—rove
beetles, carrion beetles—and fed on the maggots, William's flesh too alkaline for their liking. Then parasitoid
wasps laid their eggs inside William's body. Cheese flies
and coffin flies found William as he became too dry for
maggots—their mouth hooks needing moisture in order

to attach. Chewing beetles—ham and carcass beetles—went to work on William's flesh, skin, and ligaments, leaving only his hair to be consumed by moth larvae and mites, and his bones to disintegrate.

"It is difficult to believe in the dreadful but quiet war of organic beings, going on in the peaceful woods, & smiling fields," Darwin wrote in his journal in 1839.

What a system. "Succession" is such a hopeful word. Each of these scavengers ingesting William, then others eating those that have been eating William, becoming prey for something else. Flies filled with William, eaten by birds, then shat out, fertilizing the surrounding countryside—the grasses, blackbrush, and sage. Beetles eaten by lizards, eaten by birds, eaten by larger birds. William, "pulled out and up into the world of living things," now lives everywhere—his cells, atoms—his DNA moving back and forth, up and down in the food chain, the nutrient cycle, strands in the fantastic web of life.

Succession. Life after death. William spreads across this landscape feeding the life force. This is not the "life after death" they taught me as a child. It is real and violent and beautiful.

There might be more to William than his physical cells processed through a hundred different organisms. Death strips away only the part of him that is physical and tangible. The Buddhists believe that the physical is but one of many dimensions making up our complete selves. Life force remains once everything tangible is stripped from us. Wildness remains.

Throughout my youth I pictured dying as going to sleep for a while, waking up later with all the dead people now upright for the Second Coming. Mormons don't believe in cremation because gathering dispersed ashes will be more difficult than simply rising from the grave. I can't imagine how William might be put back together. We get up from our graves and brush off the dirt and watch our entire lives—including all secret moments, including times we swore we were alone—played for all to see on some giant movie screen. We're judged and sorted into different eternal kingdoms according to the contents of that movie, where we'll spend the rest of time. The way I once understood it, even the worst of those kingdoms is better than what we have here, now, on earth. At least this is how I remember it.

Since discovering William, the number of random thoughts and events, the strange coincidences occurring in my life, have increased over what I consider "normal." Somehow, William is responsible. For a while, I assumed that William was simply fuel for my imagination. Then William shifted from being an idea sparking my imagination to a real person. I'm now comfortable having giant gaps in my understanding and nothing in my past to make sense of a dead relative suddenly showing up in my life. I talk about William with a twinkle in my eye, leaving listeners wondering if I really believe what I'm saying, which I do. Still, I feel as if I am on a raft floating in the ocean, looking for something firm to hold onto.

Believing in life after death may be akin to believing

in anything. Like rain or love. It doesn't matter if I believe that tomorrow it will rain, because tomorrow it will either rain or it won't. There are signs and sciences to suggest rain or not, but my belief, no matter how strong, is not a factor. And my believing that you love me doesn't make you love me if you don't. Believing it will rain tomorrow might alter my actions: if I'm going out I might take a jacket, an umbrella. Believing that you love me could cause me to act foolishly in your presence or stay painfully away from you.

If I believed in the life after death I grew up with, I might act more responsibly. Show more restraint. I might make painful sacrifices, hoping for at least a PG-13 rated movie of my life and an eternal kingdom with good coffee and no big box stores. But believing in life after death doesn't make it true. Either life goes on after death or it doesn't. I say it does.

I say that the dead live and that they know more than we do and that, yes, they want to help us.

Rio begins to shiver and turns back to camp. I follow, picking up small pieces of dry wood for the fire I'm eager to build in the ring I dream has been used for a thousand years. I find Rio sitting near Ford looking cold and pathetic, forlorn in the dusk-lit air, as if he knows that I completely control his comfort. I start a fire in a handful of dried tumbleweed, adding twigs and sticks of increasing size from the pile beside me until the small world we've created begins to warm. Rio lays down on a flat rock above the fire, intercepting its rising heat. I don't expect rain but set up my small tent for warmth. Once it's up and filled with my sleeping pad and bag, Rio disappears inside.

Driven by hunger or the smell of the spices in my Tasty Bite dinner, he emerges and we both eat. He sneaks back to the tent. I feed the fire.

The fire absorbs all my attention. Flames curl and dance, furl and unfurl, the coals throb with heat, vibrating with one hundred shades of red. The past and future disappear.

Without thinking, I pick up one of the sticks meant for the fire and with it scratch random lines in the dirt next to me. I recognize these lines. I've seen them before.

I imagine Charles Darwin scratching in the dirt with a similar stick on that June day in 1837. According to his letters, he was making a "short visit to Shrewsbury." He arrived by coach from London the night before, having dinner with his family and talking with his father late into the night. The next morning he woke early and began writing in his Notebook B, in which he developed his understanding of transmutation and his search for the answer to his question, Where do species come from? After a few hours of this and breakfast, he needs a walk. Although he believes his looks haven't changed in the years since last living in Shrewsbury, familiar people he meets in the Frankwell neighborhood treat him as if he were a stranger when he passes and nods. "All the better," he says to himself, as he's not in the mood for random conversation. He's deep in thought, searching for the next marker on his path of discovery. Continuing down Drinkwater Street, he wonders if William Williams is still making furniture for old man Owen and detours toward Copthorne Road. One day during the weeks after the *Beagle* returned, Darwin ran into William in a pub and they'd caught up a bit. When he recalled that meeting, Darwin realized that he'd rambled on endlessly about what he'd seen and thought during those five years aboard the *Beagle*. William hadn't gotten a word in edgewise but hadn't really tried. Although their lives were perched at opposite ends of the political, economic, and intellectual spectrums, they got along and always seemed grateful to be together. Around William, Darwin could be himself, not who he was always expected to be. William found Darwin fascinating, and since meeting him two decades earlier, William had not only followed Darwin's life and thought but had been inspired to pay closer attention to the natural world and what it tried to tell him. Randomly meeting Darwin in the pub that night shortly after his return was perhaps the greatest hour of William's life. For days after, he recited back to himself the main story, Darwin's answer to William's question: Is there one moment from the past five years that stands out? Darwin told the story of landing at Tierra del Fuego to return his friend Jemmie Button and the others to their native home and seeing a naked "savage," dancing with his spear. Knowing how "civilized" Jemmie had become after only five years in England, Darwin realized that when compared to our long and complete history, what a "thin film" modern civilization is. That inside all of us sleeps a very wild and interesting human being.

Owen sat at his large desk going over his books when Darwin burst in.

"Owen. Charles Darwin. I don't know if you remember me, but my backside certainly knows your chairs."

"Ah, young Darwin. Nice to see you. How are your parents? I've not seen them recently. Are you here for long or have you some trip planned—a decade on the moon, this time?"

"No," Charles said, laughing. "Just back to London tomorrow to manage my notes. Does William Williams still join for you?"

"Most certainly. He'll be last to go around here. Show yourself back."

William glowed when he looked up and saw Darwin. He put down his chisel and stepped away from his bench. The four others in the large room stopped momentarily, wondering.

"How are you, young man?" Darwin said, holding out his right hand.

"How very nice to see you," William said, grabbing it.

"I can see you're busy, but I thought I'd say hello."

William took off his shop apron and laid it on his table. "I can take a minute."

"I wouldn't want that," Darwin said.

"I've been wondering what you're up to."

"Let's walk a bit." As they left, William asked Owen if he could take his break a bit early. Owen told him to take all the time he needed but didn't mean it.

Walking toward the river, Darwin did most of the talking. He heard himself thinking out loud the latest idea caught in his mind. "I think it's like this," he said, picking up a stick and scratching lines connecting to other lines in the hard dirt. "The oldest species are here, at the bottom," he said. "These are new species branching off of previous one." He explained that the segments ending in perpendicular lines represent existing species, while those without have gone extinct. William understood some of it, but Darwin pushed on, adding new information. Later that day he would add to the similar drawing he'd started in his journal, the first known drawing of the "Tree of Life."

"Are people there, on that tree?" William asked.

"I think so. Why?"

"Just that story you told me in the pub, the one about the 'savage' and your friend, Button. Where's the 'savage' on your tree? Where are we?"

"As I said, dress up the 'savage' and he is us. Strip us and we're the savage. Inside we're all the same. The differences depend on the package we're put in. Nothing more. Jemmie's people simply have no packaging.

"We're right here," Darwin said, referring to a point at the top of the drawing.

They were both quiet for a minute, staring at the

drawing, and then Darwin rubbed the drawing out with his boot.

"So," he said to William, "how are you?"

William couldn't think of anything he wanted to hear himself say, much less that Darwin might be interested in. "More birds nesting in my birdhouses than I remember. Two new beetles by the river I can't identify. Not much. Better be getting back to work. You know old Owens."

"That, I do," said Darwin.

"On that drawing," William asked as they walked, "where then does God fit? And Adam and Eve?"

Darwin felt himself stretching and his neck heating up. He'd known the possibility of this and that it was a dangerous and difficult path. Was he ready to make the first step? Would he ever be ready?

"They're on a different drawing," he said, in a tone meant to end the conversation.

Then Darwin talked about living in London and when he might be back next until they reached the shop.

"Fantastic seeing you," William said. "Never hesitate to drop by when you're in town."

"I'll see you again," Darwin said, fairly certain that he would. Although he thought it, he didn't say, "About humans on that drawing, let's keep that between us."

Without moving from my perch, I strategically place the last sticks on the fire. Rio growls when I push him aside to make room in the tent. He probably forgot for

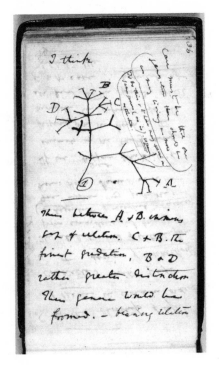

From Darwin's Notebook B, 1837

a second that this is my tent and he is damn lucky to be sleeping there. A few minutes of negotiation and manipulation and we're both comfortable. He's warmed the small space with his little body. Outside the air is still. The fire squeaks as it cools. Pronghorn must be close—I can hear their short grunts. Four coyotes chatter in the distance.

I don't sleep well, but then my body doesn't usually adapt to sleeping on the ground until the third night. Plus, Rio stunk up the tent. He has taken his last Tasty Bite.

In the morning after some food, Rio and I find our way along the base of this formation—the Rattlesnake Cliffs. We look for the opening we will follow up through to the other side where the Sweetwater River has nearly looped back on itself before cutting a narrow swath through this solid granite. From the horizontal valley, these cliffs rise only a hundred feet. Oddly, I think about icebergs: surely what I can see and touch is only a fraction of what exists down below. I can easily imagine that these cliffs are rising slowly out of the earth, breaking through the landscape decimated by overgrazing, cut into pieces by roads and fences, littered by rusted vehicles and machines, odd pipes and valves, dug by miners hoping for uranium. Someday, continuing to rise and expand, they will overcome all remnants of a time folded back into history, existing only in the dead memories of those few who believed that subduing wildness was not only their right but their responsibility: doing what they swear was the will of their god who is not my god.

We move quickly. Rio is ahead. We dodge rock outcrops and juniper trees, hop small streams, looking to our right for an opening into the wild center of these rocks. To the left, a huge flatbed pickup pulling a backhoe on a long trailer lurches along a washboarded road, followed by a solid train of dust. All its parts have come loose, based on the shattered silence. I turn a corner and suddenly Rio is perched on a rock above me. He has found the opening we've been looking for.

A split in the rocks exposes a small canyon. Our pace slows and the thinking, searching, hoping part of my brain shuts down and suddenly I'm open, waiting for whatever comes next. We follow fresh deer tracks and pass a flat rock upon which a week or a month ago a coyote squatted and shat. Fresh grasses line the deer trail and invisible birds flutter deep inside a mountain mahogany's thick foliage. Wildness bends and shifts time before compressing it into moments. Soon, my chest will open and I will mix with my wild surroundings, my own wildness bubbling to the surface to meet these rocky granite cliffs as they rise up out of the earth.

Contrary to the negative impressions many people have about the word *wild*, I feel no aggression or fear or threat in a wild place. I feel safe, in control, open. Everything around me has important information. The word *essential* comes to mind. Not in terms of this contentment being "imperative and necessary," though I would argue that it is, but actually the essence of the way life should feel, as if I've dropped into place, gears meshing, registered. As if I'm one of a trillion elements making up the life force pushing, adapting, moving. Darwin's tree of life flourishes and thickens and new leaves appear.

I follow Rio crease to crease through the granite maze. He seems to know what he is looking for, where he is going. There are intimate grottos I'd love to camp in some day. One flat stone ledge we cross is so perfect that in a different country I would believe it was placed by Roman road builders or by Aztecs at the base of a pyramid. I glance wall to wall, expecting ancient rock art, but we're moving too fast, carried inside a swift invisible flow. The cliffs divide and suddenly the valley beyond spreads out before us. Below the Sweetwater River slowly snakes and twists, its subtle surface currents glinting silver in the morning sun. A white pelican floats silently at the edge.

Somewhere exactly within this view, William Williams died.

I sit on a small granite boulder next to a miraculous blanket-sized patch of shooting stars, each one a floating red explosion.

Rio sits next to me, content to gather light in his bright white chest. We share a piece of jerky and I take three gulps of water, swallow two and spit the third into his mouth. I'm not alone in believing that in the wilderness we are our highest selves.

Rio is definitely his highest self out here. I'm sure if he has one at all, his civilized, domesticated shell is a porous, nearly transparent membrane. I know because I can see clearly through it, directly into his heart.

According to my maps the Mormon Trail keeps to the south side of the Sweetwater between Devil's Gate, twenty miles east, and here. The trail could have crossed the river north of where the highway is today—Crossing Number One. I can see how it would have hugged the river to avoid the deep sand and crossed again where the river begins snaking through the Rattlesnake Cliffs—Crossing Number Two. And I see where a bridge has since been built—Crossing Number Three.

The wind picks up, pushing cloud clumps around in the sky like ships in a crowded harbor. We find our way to the river and follow it along the base of the cliff for an eighth of a mile where it begins looping back and forth across a wide plain. William is buried near here.

Two raven acrobats play clacking in the breeze while two more pace the ground ten feet away, as if seeing to it that I obey all the rules. Rio is in heaven. But then he seems to carry heaven with him wherever he goes. I can't see him or hear the jangle of his tags but know he's nearby.

The small chance that William's bones might still lie intact multiplied by the size of the area I would need to search make the task of finding his body seem impossible. This may be as close as I get.

I'll bet I'm his first relative to visit him at his final resting place. This past Memorial Day, members of my family made the pilgrimage to the Salt Lake City Cemetery and laid wreaths and flowers on the twelve matching gray headstones perfectly aligned across the perfect lawn. My mother's grave, the most recent, is at the south end, closest to the road. Her headstone has a dark stain on it from the lit candle I placed there and let burn too long.

John George's journal makes no mention of any ceremony, marker, or prayer for God to protect and watch over William's body. Assuming it's not too late, I find a rock, longer than wide and light-colored. I tilt it upright, pressing it into the soft ground until it will stand on its own. It becomes a stone.

A few feet away, I find a good spot to sit on the ground against a downed tree. I have a clear view of the wide plain and the stone I've just placed upright. I'm too low to see the river, but from where I sit it sounds like a huge snake moving across dry land. Here with the sun warming me at a perfect angle, a nap seems nearby. Rio's nose leads him around trotting and intent as if he's on an assignment.

I watch the clouds and I wonder what birds rustle in the bush behind me. I try dissolving a small pain in my left hip by attacking it with my full attention. I doze and then wake up mid-dream in which ghostlike Mormons surround me and oxen pulling wagons still dripping from crossing the Sweetwater River move silently past. Their clothes are worn and ragged. Some walk barefooted. Many limp. They are thin and listless. Transparent children and dogs move past me, silent. A woman turns toward me, nodding acknowledgment through her dark, vacant eyes.

William is buried nearby.

Of the thousands of weary Saints that passed by here, I'll bet that not one turned to the next and said, "Too bad we weren't born one hundred years from now—we could have flown."

No one imagined flying.

Someone in the distance is singing:

Come Come Ye Saints,
No Toil or labor fear But with joy wend your way.
Though hard to you this journey may appear,
Grace shall be as your day.
Tis better far for us to strive Our useless cares from us to
*   drive;*
Do this, and joy your hearts will swell—
All is well! All is well!

Out in the future is something we have not yet imagined—something that could save us. How can we begin to imagine what might save us?

This could be what William Williams has come back to tell me.

Although the ground I've been sitting on seemed dry at first, my butt is damp and cold and I need to get up. I yell for Rio and he's back by my side before I can get my pack on, and in a second we're moving. I've done what I came to do and now it's Rio's turn to lead. I follow him up a short slope at the base of the cliff and then tell him to find the truck. With Rio in charge, I get to dump from my mind the details—direction and schedule, goals and responsibilities—and see what my imagination might do with the extra space.

We startle four deer who move confidently away. Rio stares and pokes out his thick chest but doesn't chase, which makes me think for an instant that the task I've given him trumps his fierce internal hunter. Normally Rio would find our original route and take us back the way we'd come, but I'm excited that he's taking us higher toward the center of the cliffs.

Rio moves through a space between huge boulders, too for me, and I find a different route by climbing up and around. He is kind enough to wait for me in a world of grasses and mature trees surrounded on three sides by vertical rock walls. He finds a game trail and follows it through an opening in the cliffs and onto a long ledge.

I move with little effort, not trying to keep up, carried along by an invisible current, a force. By life force.

Rio is nowhere to be seen, but I sense from the fresh tracks in mud that he's headed for the truck. I think about testing him—stopping and waiting to see how long it would be before he realizes that I might be lying somewhere with a broken ankle or a heart attack and come to save me. I'm afraid that I'd be disappointed, knowing that there is little if any Lassie in that dog.

I work my way down through the last monster boulders and out on the flat where I can see my truck. Somewhere underneath it, Rio is stretched out, asleep.

The Mormon and Oregon Trails cross the Continental Divide at South Pass "on a gentle grade that was easy on the wagons" according to journals kept by the Saints. Driving back I decide to stop there and walk along a section of the trail and get a sense of this pass, "so broad and so level that many [emigrants] did not realize they had passed into the Pacific watershed." This is as desolate country as I've ever been in—too much even for sage, and the blackbrush survives in small clumps that, if I squint, blend in with the billions of black stone fists that line the ruts defining the trail. The group, including John George and his mother, passed by here within days of burying William at Three Crossings. The wind picks up as Rio and I start along the trail. Nothing alive is even a foot tall, suggesting that wind is always here, is born here before spreading out to blow periodically everywhere else in the world. Rio moves side to side across the trail, stopping to examine the rocks or plants or old bones that attract him like a magnet. He stays closer than normal, knowing he doesn't want to be too far away when I decide that this walk is too miserable and turn back to the truck. He keeps looking up at me as if to say, "Isn't this enough?"

A dozen ravens fly by close overhead, each one riding its own wave of wind. They seem to be using their wings only to maintain their position and direction and not for propulsion—much as a boatman uses his oars in a rapid on a wild river. They dip and surge overhead, passing quickly and effortlessly through the distance between us and the trail ahead of us where they disappear. I imagine their ancestors, the same immortal wind flinging them above the heads of my ancestors making their way toward Utah. I hear wooden wheels squeak and the sounds oxen make when they work and the banging of a metal pot against a wagon's side. By this point emigrants have traveled over nine hundred miles. Although they are tired and worn down, a rhythm can be detected, a difficult ease, as if their bodies have become fluid across that distance. They gaze down and slightly in front with the vacant stare suggesting that their souls have yet to catch up.

One small bird twitters low in the brush next to me, waiting for the next hole in the wind to fly through. Wispy clouds hang above like white flags frozen in midwave. Heat on my neck suggests that the sun has overcome the wind chill and I feel the presence of pronghorn. I sense that William, knowing what death has taught him about life, would love to trade places with me. I sense this from a haunting feeling—not one that scares me, but in the feeling I have of different worlds collapsing within me. He wants my body for one purpose: to act on his knowledge of what life needs right now.

Rio is lying in a quick hole he dug, sheltered from the wind. I turn around in a complete circle and, other than the stone cairn, there is nothing to filter the signals, drown the deep hum beneath the pitch of the wind, nothing in my vision that is not an elemental part of this wild place. As stark as this landscape is, it is exact. Although not officially designated Wilderness, I know that just as my beloved Southern Utah wilderness is a deep well of possibility, so is this place—where evolution is free and constant, reacting, adapting unfettered to changing conditions. I sense the natural system as it whirs and flutters, vibrates and growls, complete and effortless.

What I see—the short dark plants, the small rocks, the lone chipping sparrow—is a fraction of what is actually here: the invisible, the organisms and microorganisms, the insects and eggs and mites, the ticks, fleas, and ants. The hiding mammals and the crickets who will sing later. This landscape is exactly right. The earth's highest self, the ultimate in imagination, the current culmination of all that has come before. Here the life force is strong and free to carry this system into both the near and distant future.

Standing in the middle of all this exactness, I feel plugged in, charged. I am part of this perfect system, this force. We all are. Although harsh and stark, this wildness moves me.

The sky drops and presses in on the space around me and I feel something is about to happen. In wild systems something is always happening. Although I have never been to this place, I feel familiar; not that the place itself is familiar, but something about me is familiar. The part of me that I share with every human who ever lived is familiar. The word *intimate* gradually becomes synonymous with *infinite*, as this part of me flows down the branches and drains into the Tree trunk of Life.

The clouds move in to filter the sun, and its heat turns pathetic—no match for the wind. It's time to turn back. Rio's excitement is not enough to keep him from inspecting the same rocks and plants and bones that signaled him before.

"What's next?" I ask myself, as my wild world dissipates into practicality as we get closer to the truck. For our species—I'm not sure. The climate could be warming too quickly for us to do much about it. Doesn't every generation fear they're the last? On the other hand, I wonder if we're in the early preparatory stages of making a leap to a different cultural level. Perhaps a new way of living in the world will be foisted upon us because, in the end, we couldn't, with all our brains and technology and markets, avert the climate crisis. Or perhaps we'll figure it out. Either way means creating a new civilization. We may be on a branch of Darwin's Tree of Life that is ready to fork. We seem poised to evolve. I stop for a minute in the cold wind and scratch that same tree of life into the hard dirt with a small stick. I mark an X at the far end of our branch, from which apes and chimps branched earlier—our current position. Adding length to our current branch is certainly possible. Not on my drawing. This time I draw two forks flaring out beyond the X, into the future. I mark a C on the shorter branch, and on the longer branch I scratch a D—for the two subspecies into which we seem to be dividing. *Homo sapiens convergi* thrives on privilege and stature and sees its type as rulers of the world. *Convergi* is mostly white and masculine, with laserlike focus on profit and power all the while undermining the natural system to which it no longer feels subjected. *Convergi* calls itself

"Pro-Life," which refers not to all life—nowhere near—but to unborn children and humans who wish to be dead. This is the opposite of *Homo sapiens divergensis* who affirms all life, is feminine, and is comfortable adapting to conditions as they change, knowing that although the future is unknown, it is filled with possibility. *Divergensis* survives on creativity and imagination and integration. *Divergensis* thrives on life force, knowing that true meaning comes through efforts to protect it. True meaning is the reward for protecting, supporting, celebrating life force.

A new species means evolution.

Darwin wrote about climate change and the natural cycles of temperature as factors in natural selection. In a changing climate an organism has two choices if it is to survive: it moves or is genetically modified. Since we can't wait for our genes to save us, we are left with one choice: movement.

Darwin was referring to movement in the strictly geographic sense. If its warming home threatens its survival, an organism must move to somewhere cooler. With the current climate crisis we are already seeing different species moving to cooler climes. But what about us? We are already there. We are already everywhere.

The word *move* has a meaning beyond the physical migration of a species.

Aren't we "moved" when inspired, surprised by beauty or meaning? We are moved by a poem, a painting, a perfect piece of music when it absorbs all our attention. Aren't we opened up, exposing another world deep inside us? I was moved standing there in the wind in the awe of that moment a few minutes ago.

Movement from the outer world to the inner world may be our salvation.

Back in the truck we lurch along slowly, bumping over small rocks and in and out of the ruts cut by recent rain. In the short distance to the pavement Rio performs a balancing act on the console between my seat and his so as not to miss anything happening beyond our front bumper. We both know that the adventure ends at the pavement. He spins around twice, then curls up on my coat and is out. The Indigo Girls sing on the radio.

Perhaps I'll never be able to prove that William Williams had anything to do with the insights ranging from small flickers of understanding to screams from the inside of my brain as it explodes, or the insomnia, the tugs and pulls, the invisible obstacles as real and as difficult to ignore as gravity. I know one thing for sure: William Williams connected me to Charles Darwin. William Williams represents my personal past, the line of ancestors on the far edge of my genealogical chart. Through his work, Darwin represents my complete history—the great chain of being linking each species on the great tree of life, twig to branch to limb to trunk back to the first vibrating cell to create its own energy and then reproduce itself. I now have a different pedigree chart, not a separate one, but one extended back to my true beginnings. My true chart includes, without hierarchy, my parents and theirs, William Williams, and 10,000 generations of humans, but also *Homo heidelbergensis, Homo habilis, Australopithecus.* On my chart is *Megazostrodon*, the small insect-eating Mesozoic mammal who managed to survive the meteor that killed the dinosaurs and is believed to be one organism to which all modern humans owe deep bows of gratitude for our lives. Back from there all the way to the day that life first sparked in that muddy ooze. Darwin showed me my true past, and William Williams connected me to it.

I have an Infinite past. What about an Infinite future?

Time was long before us and will be long after us. The length of line between who we are and who we will become is unknown. Our conscious actions can extend our future or cut it short. The length of our future is at stake.

EPILOGUE

Colorado River, Dream Water

I've missed the river. We didn't get back to Castle Valley until late June, already deep summer with its fading greens, buzzing insects, rolling heat waves, throbbing blocks of silence. We missed the exotic geraniums that cover the fields with their purple color and sweet smell and the globe mallow that thrives on disturbance. The yellows are in their prime—the prince's plum and the bright blooming *Opuntia.*

The river and I have unfinished business.

Last January, wanting to see what weeks of record low temperatures had done to the Colorado River, I followed the dogs down to my favorite beach on the south bank, not far from home.

I love this place for many reasons. It is small and intimate and has a quiet eddy where I can swim. Also, my beach is wild—wild because I can believe that my friends and I are the only humans ever to visit this place. Our tracks crisscross those of birds and small rodents and lizards dragging their tails. I've watched damselflies breeding there. It is also wild because sitting there on the edge of the Colorado River, the Dome Plateau Wilderness Unit spreads out in front of me and up and over the immense Wingate Cliffs. Behind me, the Mary Jane Canyon Wilderness's softer pink, or orange—depending on the time of day—hills rise and take off vertically up the cliffs that were once part of those across the river. Sitting there, the highway behind me does not exist.

While the dogs explored a new, frozen phase of a place they loved and knew intimately, I stood quietly looking around. The beach was under a foot of snow, on which windblown tracks formed a faint map. The cliff edge behind me blocked half the sun, separating the beach into black and white. The only sound came from dogs moving between dry crisp willows, which seemed muffled and echoed, and I wondered if cold adds density to silence. Ravens with their chortling, small mammals in dry leaves, and buzzing insects were all present in their absolute absence. I hadn't waited long when the river donned its archetypal robes.

The archetypal river suggests life's journey, the passage of time, life force. For me that cold day, the presence of ice added a new dimension to that river. Standing there in the cold sunlight, I knew that, although invisible, the constant, very real river of life—call it life force—flowed deep and soundless beneath the surface.

I'd been spending most of my creative energy getting to know and understand the deep inner world. But knowing that river flowed beneath all that chaos didn't matter. That day the river's surface demanded all my attention.

Downstream, the cold, white surface was solid, intact—no evidence of the river flowing beneath, of any inner world. Today many refuse to acknowledge that this other world exists. I'd been downstream before, completely cut off from any inner life. Some are aware of this inner world but see it as a remnant of some ancient, irrelevant past, and any mention of it in serious discussions is seen as softheaded. Others see it as dark and infernal, a place to avoid at all costs. The modern world thinks it is better off without the inner world, which it can't control. In modern life, this inner world is bad for business.

Upstream the strong current created a small channel through the ice. The inner and outer world moved together, meshed with the solid and liquid. The Life Force was there, tangible and visible, the combined inner and outer world calm, constant, and strong. Perhaps this is the world all life was born to—no separation between the inner and outer world.

In front of me, total chaos—my own chaotic surface—the ice of the modern, outer world breaking up, heaving and buckling as moving ice ground against the solid and foundational, as the deep inner river probed for weak points in the ice, forcing its way to the surface.

Until that day on the bank of that frozen river, I thought my work had been to personally discover this inner world and describe what I saw there. But acknowledging and reporting weren't enough. I needed to jump in and immerse myself.

The dogs wake me early. Although we're just past the solstice, the days seem shorter than they should with the rising sun needing extra time to clear Adobe Mesa.

I spend the morning settling back in—unpacking, reshelving a box of books, throwing away most of the mail. Why is water running off the roof? An easily fixed problem with the swamp cooler. By following the smell I discover that a poor mouse has trapped itself and died in a bucket. In the afternoon I head to the river with Rio and Winslow, the rat terrier-chihuahua we recently rescued. We've waited all winter and then all spring.

The path is overgrown—the squawbush and sage doing well, but so is the exotic knapweed. The tunnel through the tamarisk and willows is invisible with all the new growth inside it. But Rio knows the way and plunges through. Winslow and I follow.

High water has shrunk the beach. The river is not the flood it was a few years back but still strong, still fast. The small willows I remember have exploded in size. The dogs race around like they've been let out of jail.

The river is green and clouded. Without testing it, I know the water is cold. I know I have to jump in.

I've been in the river a hundred times, but back before it became a metaphor. This will be different.

I've made some progress these past months, and,

like exercise, a lot of it hurt. I've burned inside thinking about the early years I spent focused on being the best modern American man I could, then discovering that wasn't me—knowing who I wasn't but not sure who I was. I've learned a phrase for the experiences I've had in my inner world. "Second attention" comes from the Toltecs in Mexico, but shamans throughout the world use it. First attention is what we notice and respond to daily. We use it to deal with life's mundane details in order to function in society. In first attention, life is an orderly sequence of events along a linear timeline. If the first attention is what we think with our brains, our second attention comes from our bodies. Time loses stature in our second attention and so does money. Carlos Castaneda calls second attention non-ordinary awareness due to its dreamlike qualities. Second attention experiences are often ineffable and discounted by our first attention, if we let them be.

The rational, first attention can't create anything new. Second attention may be the only path toward meaningful change.

This is true for me. The thousands of painful hours I've spent planning, strategizing, budgeting, thinking haven't amounted to much. The important things in my life have surprised me, come out of the blue, up from my inner world, out of my second attention. Second attention does not plan or strategize or think. The rocks and stones in Solitude Wash, the painting in Paris. The bones in Recapture and the stars in the San Rafael Desert. A revelation at the Sweetwater River. None of it planned. All of it remarkable. It's clear now: William Williams comes to me via my second attention. Dragonflies appearing signal me to pay second attention.

Time stops while I stand looking at the cold river. A dragonfly nearby hangs suspended, floating in thick air. I've experienced second attention though only through glimmers of light or a hum or throb coming in from behind or to the side of me. Or a shadow with nothing to form the shadow, with no source. Sometimes, I think, second attention comes to me when I react to something my brain can't make sense of, a decision or choice I cannot explain, which in the future turns out to be pure and right.

Second attention, I think, stripping down as an invisible breeze chills my bare skin, might be the earth telling us how it can make the best use of us.

I'm hoping that somehow submerging myself in this cold river will be a symbolic and ritualistic act, one that will move me closer to knowing my own essence—how I'm "essential" to the future, in the same way that all biological organisms are essential to the future. I think about taking a running leap into the water. I sense that this act will be the end of one thing and the beginning of something else. I am about to leap when a voice—William Williams?—stops me: "Better you just ease in," it says.

Taking that advice, I walk to the river's edge and step in. The more weight I transfer from my dry foot to my wet one, the deeper into the cold mud I sink. I step out with my other foot, same thing. Knowing that too much time on one foot might get me stuck, I keep moving. The river has changed. I take ten steps toward the middle and the water level still does not reach my knees. The freezing water numbs my legs. The river should be nipple deep by now. I need to finish this up before freezing to death in water that has come 500 miles and dropped 9,000 feet in the week since it was snow. I move ten yards toward the middle of the river into waist-deep water.

Rather than quickly submerging myself in order to get it over with, I instinctively pinch my nose with my right thumb and forefinger. Then I grab my right wrist with my left hand. This is how I remember being baptized in a church font, fifty-two years before. My father's hands are missing—his right one supporting my back, and his left holding my right as he tilted me into the warm water.

Leaning upstream I am being held: either the current holds me, or William Williams.

The key with Mormon baptism is to leave the child submerged only as long as it takes the witness to verify that his entire body is immersed. This time, as I fall back I open my eyes to look up. I am in no hurry to leave that depth. I no longer feel the cold. At first, nothing but blackness above, but slowly the silt clears and the darkness dissolves, exposing a tube of muted daylight directly over me. I watch the current move as floating particles weave and twist between the light and me. There is no tightness in my chest as I hold my breath. This second baptism becomes my commitment to my second attention, to being open to every necessary, essential, deep unconscious element as it rises to the surface of my life. A dream I had that winter comes back to me—I was underwater, at the bottom of a deep well. I was afraid, not knowing whether it was dream water or real water, because breathing in real water would drown me. It was dream water.

Acknowledgments

I acknowledge:

The great hearts at SUWA: Richard, Scott, Scott, Steve, Matt, Diane, Anne, Neal, Heidi, Liz, Deeda, Clayton, David, Dave, Terri, Gina, Jen, Jackie, and Ray, for showing me his maps.

Janet Browne, who brought Darwin to life in her books, and for her referring to *civilization* as a "thin film." Steve Defa, who helped me make sense and who introduced me to the work of Arnold Mindell, which opened me to my "second attention." Martha Lucy and John Gurche, who helped me understand Cain's body. Vance Martin of Wild.org knew C. A. Meier and invited him to speak in Scotland in 1983, and later published the book about it, *A Testament to Wilderness.* Mike Matz, who first uttered the phrase "we save the wilderness because it saves us." And John Berger, for "the proverbial nature of stones" and much, much more.

The Bainbridge Graduate Institute (especially Gifford Pinchot III, Libba Pinchot, Jill Bamberg, Aly Tibbetts, April Atwood, John Ehrenfeld, and Tom Johnson), for introducing me to the practicality of the inner world during my MBA program. The original proposal for this book was my final project.

The Mesa Refuge, where I wrote an early draft, and am honored by the company my book will keep in the library of that miraculous place.

Brothers in the struggle: Chris Noble, Nick Sichterman, Bob Helmes, Bob Schuster, Rick Bass, Todd Wilkinson, Toby McLeod, Vaughn Hadenfeldt, Mark Bailey, Mark Meloy, Bill Hedden, Andy Nettel, Jim Campbell, Dave Mock, OB O'Brien, Michael Peck, Robert Newman, Jeff Foott, Jonathan Schecter, Scott Berry, Ed Riddell, David Nimkin, John Taft, Rob Shetterly, Frank Carter, Lucas St. Clair, John Milliken, Ian Cumming, Doug Schnitzspahn, Chris Peterson, Peter Lawson, Damian Bollerman, Floyd Wilkes, Doug Bennett, Steve Barker, Gavin Noyes, George Wuerthner, Gil Williams, Tim Petersen, Tim DeChristopher, Glen Lathrop, Scott Slovic, Dennis Sizemore, Steve Tatum, Mark Austin, Rob Mrowka, Bill Resor, Dave Foreman, Larry Clarkson, Bruce Hucko, Dave Lyle, Scott Wood, and Scott Hinckley.

Sisters who have, directly or indirectly, taken on the difficult task of nurturing my anima (how Jung referred to the woman in a man), my feminine: Carol Kaza, Sonya Campion, Becky Thomas, Jenepher Stowell, Laura Kamala, Ariel Muller, Eleanor Hedden, Sarah Hedden, Chloe Hedden, Christy Williams, Lyn Dalebout, Vicky Newman, Sue Halpern, Lee Riddell, Geralyn Dreyfous, Story Clark, Trent Alvey, Sandy Mailliard, Kirsten Johanna Allen, Joan

DeGiorgio, Mary O'Brien, Giovannina Anthony, Andrea Peacock, Kinde Nebecker, Laura Cameron, Judith Zimmerman, Melody Taft, Monica Woelfel, Louisa Carter, Patricia Hasbach, Betsy Burton, Annette Cumming, Anne Hinckley, Anne Milliken, Ann Krcik, Ann Backer, Anne Wilson, Mariah Hughes, Alexandra Fuller, Rebecca Solnit.

Castle Valley kindred spirits: Dave Erley, Yrma van der Steenstraeten, Brian Murray, Janie Tuft, Glenn Kincaid, Tana Kincaid, Stoke Dutton, Tory Hill, Mitch Stock, Bob Lippman, Pam Hackley.

Our Eastern family, Terry Osborne, Andy Friedland, Katie Friedland, MK Beach, Hillary Joy Beach, Jacob Osborne, Anne Kapuscinski, Wayne Barstad, Gus Speth, Cameron Speth, Mary Evelyn Tucker, Kim Wind, Rosie Kerr, John Grimm, Christina Seely, Ross Virginia, Doug Bolger, Celia Chen, Jenna Musco, David Peart, Carol Folt, Mark McPeek.

Students past and present (University of Utah, Dartmouth, the Murie Center), for the roles they've played in opening my mind.

Nieces, nephews, grandnieces, and grandnephews, for the pieces we leave behind that you'll be picking up. God-daughter, Annabelle Milliken, god-son, Quinn Carter.

High Desert Journal's "Moving Stones," which became chapter 3, "Solitude Wash"; and *Whitefish Review*'s "That Wildman Cain," which became chapter 8, "Musée d'Orsay, Paris."

Bret Webster, for his deep love of wildness and his cover photo.

Madi Quissek, for holding everything together.

Mercedes Ornelas, for order.

Mentors: Doug Peacock, Yvon Chouinard, W.S. Merwin, Jack Turner, Bill McKibben, Tom Campion, Peter Metcalf, Bill Hedden, Randall Tolpinrud. And Eleanor Hedden, Adele Alsop, Meredith Sabini. And Scarlett Kinney, my teacher and guide to other significant worlds.

The important deaths and lives of Peter Matthiessen, Jim Harrison, and John Anderson.

The perfect tension Louis Gakumba uses to tune this old guitar.

Conversations with and support and love from my father, Rex Williams, and my stepmother, Shirley.

The firm and honest balance provided by Terry's father, John, and Jan Sloan for infinite quantities of both books and grace.

My siblings: Joe, Jann, Tom, Amy, Becky, Nan, Steve.

Terry's siblings: Dan, Hank, Anne. And all her amazing cousins.

Henry Thayer, my agent, who watched out for me and helped construct this last version.

Tom Payton, Daniel Simon, Sarah Nawrocki, Burgin Streetman, Rebecca Lown, and the folks at BookMatters, for their professionalism, commitment to books, and their roles in making this book real.

But especially Barbara Ras, for her belief and sup-